PROPHETIC LITERATURE

VERY REV. PETER SAMUEL KUCER, MSA

En Route Books and Media, LLC
St. Louis, MO

⚓ENROUTE
Make the time

En Route Books and Media, LLC
5705 Rhodes Avenue
St. Louis, MO 63109

Cover credit: TJ Burdick

Library of Congress Control Number: 2020944488

ISBN-13: 978-1-952464-26-3

Acknowledgments

I would particularly like to acknowledge Very Rev. Edward Przygocki, M.S.A., U.S.A., Province Provincial of the Missionaries of the Holy Apostles, who gave me permission to publish.

Special thanks also to Dr. Sebastian Mahfood, O.P., President of En Route Books and Media, for publishing this work.

Contents

Introduction

It is important not to confuse prophecy with what is classified in the Bible as prophetic books. Some and not all the prophets of the Old Testament have books that bear their names. For example, the

---

prophecies of Elijah and Elisha are contained in the two books of kings and not in separate books named after them. In addition, the gift of prophecy did not end with the Old Testament but continued in the New Testament and is still given today. The difference between biblical prophecy and non-biblical prophecy, explains Scott Hahn, is that the biblical:

> canonical prophets that we find in the Old Testament gives us a norm, not an exclusionary norm that prevents further prophecy of course. In fact, the norm that the Old Testament prophets give us is referential and Christological in its reference. It points to the definitive disclosure, when the Word of God became man. Suddenly, all the prophecy comes to a point of fulfillment, but not termination. It isn't as though suddenly prophecy ceased and the need for it. It isn't with the fulfilment that Christ brought about that prophecy ceased in the sense it is over and done with because Christ has brought it to an end, Christ has fulfilled it. What Christ has done in fulfilling it is what he has done with the law "It is not that I have come to abolish the Law and the prophets I have come to fulfill the law and the prophets." So now we see the expansion of the truth that was gained by the prophets for all the world, not just to Israel, but to all the nations as well. And so the need for the study of the prophets is very great. The need for the gift of prophecy in order to study and understand the prophets is no less important.[2]

---

[2] Scott Hahn, *Your Share of the Prophets: A Study of the Old Testament Prophecy* (Saint Joseph Communications), MP3, disk 1.

With this broader understanding of prophecy as pointing to Christ and fulfilled in Christ[3] and, consequently, a gift that is given in all ages and time we will now direct our attention to the canonical prophetic literature that follows wisdom literature. This prophetic literature is in continuity with the preceding wisdom literature. Both teach perennial moral truths that reflect how God has created the universe, in particular how God created human beings as inherently social creatures who are to reflect God's image and likeness. Since only God is absolutely holy the prophets, points out Gordon J. McConville, are at times portrayed as failing to live up to their call to holiness. Through Hosea, God says that like certain disreputable priests, the prophet "also shall stumble with you by night (Hosea 4:5 *RSVCE*)". Similarly, Jeremiah laments, "Both prophet and priest are ungodly; even in my house I have found their wickedness (Jeremiah 23:11 *RSVCE*)".[4]

When the prophets act in accordance with their vocation of proclaiming timeless divine truth, they do so in two primary ways, explains McConville: denouncing idolatry, and encouraging the practice of justice and righteous behavior, in particular among their people chosen by God to lead all nations to God. [5] As the prophets,

---

[3] Hahn defines prophecy as "the typological interpretation of history." Scott Hahn, *Your Share of the Prophets,* MP3.

[4] Gordon J. McConville, *Exploring the Old Testament: A Guide to the Prophets: 4 Exploring the Bible Series* (Downers Grove: InterVarsity Press, 2002), xiv.

[5] McConville, xix.

continues McConville, give way to their divinely inspired prophetic impulse, they develop biblical terminology by including nations other than Israel in key terms, including covenant and Israel. As will be seen, Isaiah includes non-Israelites in the term covenant, and prophecies a day when representatives from the Gentile nations will join Israel in worship of God.[6]

The content of the prophetic message of the prophets encompasses past, present, and future. With respect to the past, prophets remind people of a moral and faith standard that is undiluted by compromises accumulated by the passage of time.[7] The present is of utmost importance since the prophetic message is directed, but not exclusively, to the people of the prophet's time. Sometimes this means that the directives of one prophet will differ from another prophet's directives which are given at another time. For example, comments Miller, "in one century, the prophet Isaiah tells the king not to surrender to the besieging army, God will defend his people. In the next century, the prophet Jeremiah tells the king to surrender to the besieging army, because God has chosen to punish us."[8] Ultimately, explains Miller, Isaiah and Jeremiah are prophesying in the same way since they are directing the people to follow God's will. The prophecies differ in the application of God's will which is affected by changing circumstances. When applying God's will to a specific time the prophets inspire others and at times direct others to carry out God's

---

[6] McConville, xxiv.

[7] Benedict XVI, *Dogma and Preaching: Applying Christian Doctrine to Daily Life*, trans. Michael J. Miller (San Francisco: Ignatius Press, 2011), 16.

[8] Robert D. Miller II, *Understanding the Old Testament* (Chantilly: The Teaching Company, 2019), 212.

will be reforming their lives and the nation's life. Understood in this way, Miller explains, "the prophets are not themselves reformers … [T]hey are not going to tear down pagan altars. They're going to preach to others to do so. … [T]hey're going to preach about injustice. … [T] are the conscience of Israel not its reformers."[9]

Finally, the future is included by the message's applicability to people in the future, and by predictions of the future. Whether or not the predicted future events will take place is typically conditioned by how the people of Israel repent or fail to repent. This gift of prophecy with respect to how the present will unfold, teaches Benedict XVI, is not to be understood as clear visions of future events but rather as the God given ability:

> to know an inner logic, the logic of God, within apparently chance happenings. Even if this does not enable us to predict what is going to happen at this or that point, nonetheless we may develop a certain sensitivity for the dangers contained in certain things – and for the hopes that are in others. A sense of the future develops, in that I see what destroys the future – because it is contrary to the inner logic of the road – and what, on the other hand, leads onward – because it opens the positive doors and corresponds to the inner design of the whole. To that extent the ability to diagnose the future can develop. It's the same with the prophets. They are not to be understood as seers, but as voices who understand time from God's point of

---

[9] Miller, 212.

view and can therefore warn us against what is destructive –
and, on the other hand, show us the right road forward.[10]

Another way that prophets represent God's timeless wisdom is by
representing the fulness of truth and not an aspect of truth that is
divorced from other aspects of truth. In so doing, prophets challenge
their listeners, especially those who are confident they are living
upright lives. Prophets not only urge individuals to recognize the sins
they have ignored by also direct their prophecies to their countrymen
as a whole as, writes Miller, "the conscience of the nation."[11]

In calling both individuals and the nation to conversion, writes
Abraham J. Heschel, "The prophets had disdain for those to whom
God was comfort and security; to them God was a challenge, an
incessant demand. He is compassion, but not a compromise; justice,
but not inclemency."[12]

As voices for God, Brant Pitre comments, the prophets prepared
the way for the incarnation of truth, for the future king of the tribe of
Judah who as the Messiah, as God's anointed one, will restore King
David's kingdom. This king will also usher in the time of a new
Exodus, when the scattered tribes of Israel would be re-united and

---

[10] Benedict XVI, *Day by Day with Pope Benedict XVI*, ed. Peter John
Cameron (San Francisco: Ignatius Press, 2006), 42.

[11] Miller, 211.

[12] Abraham J. Heschel, *The Insecurity of Freedom: Essays on Human
Existence* (New York: Farrar, Straus & Giroux, 1967), 11.

worship God in new temple, according to a new law and a new covenant by which all of creation is renewed.[13]

In this new era, God will perfect the institution of Israel, the laws that bind Israel together, and Israel's worship. Consequently, the criticism that the prophets directed towards priesthood, cult, sacrifice, law, institution and even towards themselves ceases as the various roles God assigns to people are brought into harmony with another in accordance with God's original intention.

Section Questions

1. Name two prophets who are mentioned in the books of Kings and who do not have books named after them. The first was assumed into heaven in a fiery chariot. Afterward, the second prophet continued the mission of this prophet.
2. How specifically, according to McConville, do prophetic terms become more inclusive especially the terms Covenant and Israel?
3. Why does Miller describe prophets as not primarily reformers and how do the prophets act as a conscience, collectively and

---

[13] Brant Pitre, *The Old Testament-A Historical and Theological Journey through Jewish Scripture Outline*, 58-65. Pitre cites: Isaiah 11; Jeremiah 3, 23, 30-31; Ezekiel 36-37; Daniel 9; Micah 5-7; Zechariah 9-10; Hosea 1-2; Micah 4; Isaiah 11, 56, 66; Jeremiah 3, 23; Ezekiel 36-37; Tobit 13-14; Deuteronomy 30; Hosea 1-2; Isaiah 11, 40; Jeremiah 3, 23; Ezekiel 20; Zechariah 10; See Micah 4; Isaiah 2; Jeremiah 30-31; See Micah 3-4; Isaiah 56, 65-66; Ezekiel 40-48; See Hosea; Jeremiah 30-31; Ezekiel 36-37; Daniel 9. 139 See Isaiah 25-27; 65-66; Ezekiel 36-37; Daniel 12

individually understood?

4. With respect to practice and worship what specifically do the prophets condemn?

5. How does Miller explain that Isaiah and Jeremiah are not contradicting one another when Isaiah tells the king not to surrender and Jeremiah tells another king to surrender?

Isaiah

Introduction

Isaiah's name in Hebrew is *yeshiyahu* (יְשַׁעְיָהוּ) and means salvation of the LORD (*yah*, an abbreviation for Yahweh), or the LORD (God) saves.[1] As one who reveals divine salvation, Isaiah is the one of prophets classified in Catholicism as one of the four major prophets: Isaiah, Jeremiah, Ezekiel and Daniel. The four are followed by Twelve Minor Prophets: Hosea, Joel, Amos, Obadiah, Jonah, Micah, Nahum, Habakkuk, Zephaniah, Haggai, Zechariah, and Malachi.

Modern scholarship typically divides the book of Isaiah into two parts and then subdivides the second part into two sections. The major division consists of chapters one through thirty-nine and chapters forty through sixty-six. The second part then is further divided and consists of chapters forty through chapters fifty-five and chapters fifty-six through chapters sixty-six.

The major difference between part one and part two is that part one appears in large part to be centered on the late 700s B.C. when Assyria was threatening to overtake the southern Kingdom of Judah. The second part complements the first by appearing to focus, but not exclusively, on a few centuries later, the 500s B.C., during the time and after the time when the Babylonians had conquered the Kingdom of

---

[1] "3470. Ysha'yah, Strong's Concordance," biblehub.com, https://biblehub.com/hebrew/3470.htm.

Judah and exiled many of its people.

The main difference that Bergsma and Pitre highlight between the two sections of the second part of Isaiah is that while chapters forty through chapters fifty-five focus on the redemption of Israel, referred to as Zion, the mountain where Jerusalem is located, in chapters fifty-six through sixty-six there is a greater apparent emphasis on the redemption of Gentiles along with God's chosen people.[3]

In comparing the different parts of Isaiah to movements within one symphony, Miller artfully explains how even though the different sections may have their "own historical context...the book as a whole

---

[2] Gustave Doré [Public domain], "The Prophet Isaiah (Is. 1:1-7,16-31)," https://commons.wikimedia.org/wiki/File:120.The_Prophet_Isaiah.jpg.

[3] John Bergsma and Brant Pitre, *A Catholic Introduction to the Bible, Volume I* (San Francisco: Ignatius Press, 2018), Kindle Location, 15719-15745.

is one symphony-intentionally woven together probably around 520 B.C." He continues:

> Whoever was responsible for the final form of this book knew what they were doing. While they kept the movements distinct, they put bits in the first movement that prefigure themes of the third movement; and elements in the second movement not only respond to things in the first movement but bits of the first movement were designed in their final form around those elements in the second. So, for example, when we read something in the first few chapters of Isaiah that is associated with an actual prophet named Isaiah, the hand of the final editor of 520 BCE is also at work there.[4]

In contrast with the view that Isaiah was written by multiple authors, traditionally the book of Isaiah has been at least attributed to Isaiah.[5] Internal data that lends support to the traditional view, comment Bergsma and Pitre, include that that later part of the book of Isaiah is similar to the first part of Isaiah with respect to "diction and theme" and both parts refer to the time of the 500s Babylonian exile and not just the second part.[6] The references to the Babylonian exile by a prophet who lived in the around two years before they occurred

---

[4] Robert D. Miller II, *Understanding the Old Testament* (Chantilly: The Teaching Company, 2019), 255.

[5] Bergsma and Pitre, Kindle Location, 16245. The following is cited: Mt 13:14-15, Jn 12:39-41, Mt 3:3, Jn 1:23, Mt 12:17, Jn 12:38, Mt 8:17, Acts 8:28, Lk 4:17, Rom 10:20-21.

[6] Bergsma and Pitre, Kindle Location, 16326. See Isaiah 2, 13-14, 34-35.

can be explained by Isaiah's prophetic gift from God who transcends time and who enables Isaiah to predict future events.

This gift of "foretelling" the future does not mean, points out McConville, that Isaiah did not also speak a prophetic message ("forthtelling") that was directly relevant to his people.[7] Likely, it will not be clearly resolved if Isaiah was written by one author, by multiple authors or by a school that ensured the book as a whole is united. However, rightly observe Bergsma and Pitre, "whatever various scholars conclude about the origins of the book of Isaiah, it is, of course, the final canonized form of the book that is theologically normative, and not various hypothetical earlier stages of composition."[8]

Section Questions

1. What does Isaiah's name in Hebrew (*Yeshiyahu*) mean? Salvation of the LORD or God Saves
2. Name the four major prophets.
3. How does the dominant modern understanding of who wrote Isaiah differ from the more traditional account? Choose either the modern understanding or the traditional account and defend its reasonableness in at least two specific ways.
4. With respect to the present and the future, distinguish between foretelling and forthtelling.

---

[7] Gordon J. McConville, *Exploring the Old Testament: A Guide to the Prophets: 4 Exploring the Bible Series* (Downers Grove: InterVarsity Press, 2002), 8.

[8] Bergsma and Pitre, Kindle Location, 16387.

5. Why do Bergsma and Pitre assert that the final canonical form of Isaiah is "theologically normative"?

Isaiah Part I Chapters 1-39: Judgment and Punishment

Chapters 1-6 Introductory Chapters

The first chapter identifies Isaiah as the "son of Amoz (Isaiah 1:1 *RSVCE*)." According to Jewish tradition, Isaiah was killed by King

---

[9] Viktor Mikhailovich Vasnetsov [Public domain], "Viktor Vasnetsov's The Last Judgment, 1904," https://commons.wikimedia.org/wiki/File: Vasnetsov_Last_Judgment.jpg.

Manasseh after Manasseh falsely accused Isaiah of teaching against the Torah. The king killed Isaiah by ordering Isaiah to be sawed in half.[10]

Chapter six, describes Isaiah beginning his ministry, "[i]n the year that King Uzziah died (Isaiah 6:1 *RSVCE*)." Bergsma and Pitre estimate that this year was 742 B.C. Based on the references given in Isaiah, they further list Isaiah prophesying during the following reigns: "1. King Uzziah (ca. 783-742 B.C.) 2. King Jotham (ca. 742-735 B.C.) 3. King Ahaz (ca. 735-715 B.C.) 4. King Hezekiah (ca. 715-687 B.C.)"[11] As stated previously, traditionally Isaiah was killed by Hezekiah's son King Manasseh, who "did what was evil in the sight of the Lord, according to the abominable, idolatrous practices of the nations" including burning "his son as an offering" to a false God (2 Kings 21:2, 6 *RSVCE*)."

Beginning in the first chapter, Isaiah strongly opposes idolatrous practices. Included in his condemnation is criticism of liturgical practices that although on the surface look as if they are directed towards God are not since the people offering them are not striving to be holy as God is holy. In order for the sacrifices to be acceptable to God, Isaiah teaches, the people are to "wash themselves; make yourselves clean; remove the evil of your doings from before my eyes; cease to do evil, learn to do good; seek justice, correct oppression; defend the fatherless, plead for the widow (Isaiah 1:16-17 *RSVCE*)." Similarly, Jesus teaches Pharisees who strictly tithed, "woe to you Pharisees! For you tithe mint and rue and every herb, and neglect

---

[10] "The William Davidson Talmud," Sefaria.org, Yevamot 49b, Sanhedrin 103b. https://www.sefaria.org/Sanhedrin.103b?lang=bi, https://www.sefaria.org/Yevamot.49b?lang=bi,

[11] Bergsma and Pitre, Kindle Location, 15755.

justice and the love of God; these you ought to have done, without neglecting the others (Luke 11:42 *RSVCE*)."

The fault that concerned both Jesus and Isaiah is not the practice of tithing or the celebration of liturgy but rather, as Bergsma and Pitre explain, the hypocrisy of tithing and/or celebrating liturgy without the corresponding love of neighbor who is made in the image and likeness of God. How can we claim to love God who we do not see if we fail to love image and likeness in our neighbor whom we do see (1 John 4:20)?[12]

In the second chapter, Isaiah prophecies that one day people from "all the nations shall flow" to the holy city of Jerusalem where God will teach them "to walk in his paths" and as a consequence there will be perfect harmony and peace as people from all nations follow God's law and "beat their swords into plowshares, and their spears into pruning hooks (Isaiah 2:4 *RSVCE*)." The very instruments of death will become transformed into instruments for bringing forth new life for God is a God of life. These instruments of death are used by men to dominate others and thereby lift themselves up high in pride, a pride that only will be "brought low (Isaiah 2:17 *RSVCE*)" since only God is truly "high and lifted up (Isaiah 6:1 *RSVCE*)" and who is lifted high up by ceaselessly affirming life, by raising life and not by killing, and not by destroying life in order to be raised higher as man is prone to do.[13]

The third through fifth chapters shifts away from the day when "men will cast forth their idols" and truly worship God to a time that will precede this perfect harmony. The time focused on is a day of judgment, punishment and consequently also an opportunity for

---

[12] Bergsma and Pitre, Kindle Location, 15779.

[13] McConville, 5.

repentance and turning back to the Lord, to right worship which necessarily entails love of neighbor, the practice of "justice [and] ... righteousness (Isaiah 5:7 *RSVCE*)" and not by, proclaims the Lord, "crushing my people by grinding the face of the poor (Isaiah 3:15 *RSVCE*)." The injustice of the wicked will eventually overtake the wicked, prophecies Isaiah, "for what his hands have done shall be done to him (Isaiah 3:11 *RSVCE*)." In other words, moral disorder will in time lead to social collapse and when this occurs the punishment of the wicked will be a fruit of their own wicked deeds.

[14] Benjamin West [Public domain], "Prophetic inspiration: Isaiah's Lips Anointed with Fire," https://commons.wikimedia.org/wiki/File: Isaiah%27s_Lips_Anointed_with_Fire.jpg.

Continuing the theme of purification, chapter six situates Isaiah in the year when King Uzziah died. In this chapter, Isaiah confesses to God that "I am a man of unclean lips" and not worthy to be a prophet. God responds by sending an angel to Isaiah who touches Isaiah's tongue with a burning coal and says "Behold, this has touched your lips; your guilt is taken away, and your sin forgiven (Isaiah 6:7 *RSVCE*)."

Chapters 7-12 The Immanuel Child

Thus purified, Isaiah in the subsequent chapter, preaches to Uzziah's son King Ahaz by telling Ahaz to trust God and not in an earthly ruler no matter how apparently powerful the ruler appears. At the time, the powerful empire whom Ahaz wanted to ally himself were the Assyrians whom Ahaz hoped would aid him in countering the northern kingdom of Israel referred to as Ephraim. The northern kingdom of Israel was in alliance with the king of Syria and Pekah.[15] With respect to worldly powers, Psalm 146 warns, "Put not your trust in princes, in a son of man, in whom there is no help ... Happy is he whose help is the God of Jacob, whose hope is in the Lord his God (Psalm 146:3, 5 *RSVCE*)." In accordance with this counsel, Isaiah counsels Ahaz and other political leaders not to be persuaded by the powerful rulers in this world who appear to be directing history since "reality" write Bergsma and Pitre, is "unfolding according to Yahweh's purpose, and so the right attitude is trust in him."[16]

---

[15] McConville, 1. McConville cites 2 Kings 16 for further details on the alliances.

[16] McConville, 5.

It is in this political context that a child named Immanuel, (עִמָּנוּאֵל), meaning God is with us, is prophesied to be born of "the virgin (Isaiah 7:8 *RSVCE*)," also translated as "the young woman (*NABRE*)." This child, along with other references to children in chapters 7-12, will one day save the people of God from their oppression, and the government of the world will "be on his shoulder (Isaiah 9:4 *RSVCE*)." St. Justin Martyr interprets the governance as foreshadowing the time when Christ will rule from the cross: "This signifies the power of the cross, which at his crucifixion, he placed on his shoulders."[17] In governing, the child will one day establish a just world-wide kingdom, and, consequently, "will be called Wonderful Counselor, Mighty God, Everlasting Father, Prince of Peace (Isaiah 9:6 *RSVCE*)."

St. John Chrysostom interpret these names as a prophecy of Jesus's divine nature. Chrysostom asks, "Did you see how both the name Lord is given to the Father and the name is given to the Son?"[18] In interpreting these verses as pointing to Christ, the Church Fathers are not claiming that Isaiah thought that these verses should be interpreted in this manner. The Church Fathers believed, argues Pitre, that Isaiah, or another writer, is not the primary author of the Book of Isaiah. This is because God is the primary author of Isaiah, as God is of the entire Bible. Since God, states Pitre, "knows exactly what He is going to do in the New Covenant" the Old Testament contains a

---

[17] Steven A. McKinion, *Ancient Christian Commentary on Scripture: Old Testament X Isaiah 1-39*, (Downers Grove, InterVarsity Press, 2004), 137. Justin Martyr's *First Apology*, 35 is cited.

[18] McKinion, 137. John Chrysostom's *Against the Anomoeans*, 5.15 is cited.

"spiritual surplus of meaning." This is, adds Pitre, "especially evident in the prophets...There is a revelatory greatness to their works that lends itself to that spiritual sense."[19]

The establishment of this kingdom will begin in the same place where people from the Northern Kingdom of Israel were first defeated and deported by the Assyrians in the early 700s B.C. Matthew's Gospel interprets this prophecy of a savior child as fulfilled in Jesus who began his public ministry of salvation, in "the land of Zebulun and the land of Naphtali (Matthew 4:15 *RSVCE*)." In a subsequent chapter, it is similarly prophesied that a child will born "from the stump of Jesse

---

[19] Brant Pitre, *The Old Testament-A Historical and Theological Journey through Jewish Scripture*, 56.

[20] Gerard van Honthorst [Public domain], "File:Gerrit van Honthorst - Adoration   of   the   shepherds.jpg," https://commons.wikimedia.org/wiki/File:Gerrit_van_Honthorst_-_Adoration_of_the_shepherds.jpg.

(Isaiah 11:1)." Jesse was the father of King David. The stump refers to the Davidic dynasty that ended when in 500s B.C. the Babylonian King Nebuchadnezzar invaded and defeated the southern Kingdom of Judea. From this cut down royal tree there will spring forth new life in the form of a Davidic child whom "the Spirit of the Lord shall rest upon him, the spirit of wisdom and understanding, the spirit of counsel and might, the spirit of knowledge and the fear of the Lord (Isaiah 11:2 *RSVCE*)."

Matthew's genealogy which traces Jesus through Joseph to King David of the tribe of Judah presents Jesus as the promised savior child. Jesus is the promised child who is filled with the gifts of the "Spirit of the Lord" that Isaiah identifies, and Christian tradition calls as the seven gifts of the Holy Spirit. St. Ambrose in stating this writes: "And let it not trouble you that either here it is said 'rivers' or elsewhere 'seven Spirits,' for by the sanctification of these seven gifts of the Spirit, as Isaiah said, is signified the fullness of all virtue; the Spirit of wisdom and understanding, the Spirit of counsel and strength, the Spirit of knowledge and godliness, and the Spirit of the fear of God. One, then is the river, but many the channels of the gifts of the Spirit. This river, then, goes forth from the fount of life."[21]

The messianic child who is filled with the gifts of the "Spirit of the LORD (Isaiah 11:2 *RSVCE*)" will usher in a new Kingdom, under His peaceful reign, where, "The wolf shall dwell with the lamb, and the leopard shall lie down with the kid, and the calf and the lion and the fatling together, and a little child shall lead them (Isaiah 11:6 *RSVCE*)." In this renewed, transformed world there will be, comments Pitre and Bergsma, "a return to the vegetarian peace that once reigned before

---

[21] McKinion, 193-194. Ambrose, *On the Holy Spirit, 1.16* is cited.

the Fall (cf. Gen 1:29-30; Gen 9:3)."[22] In peace the "remnant" of the LORD's people will gather with people from all nations in praise of God (Isaiah 11:10-16 *RSVCE*)." Unlike the exclusivity of the Exodus of old, which focused on the nation of Israel under the leadership of Moses, this "New Exodus," observe Bergsma and Pitre, is inclusive, is Catholic, open to all nations under the leadership of the new Moses, the new Joshua, Jesus Christ.[23]

The first reference to a child of salvation has since early Christian times been interpreted as fulfilled in Jesus as the child and Mary as the virgin, or young woman. Pitre argues that the apparent ambiguity of the Hebrew words *ha alma* (הָעַלְמָה) which is literally translated either as a specific virgin, the (הַ) virgin, or the young woman, is more properly translated as the virgin since in no place in the Old Testament is *alma* ever used in reference to a married woman.[24] In addition, when the Jewish people, under Greek domination around two hundred years before the birth of Christ, translated the Hebrew Scripture into Greek they chose to translate the Hebrew word *alma* with the Greek word *parthenos* (παρθένος) which when it appears in the bible contextually means virgin.[25]

To do justice to the various ways that the prophecy of the Emmanuel Child and the virgin are fulfilled, Pitre distinguishes between "preliminary fulfillment" and ultimate fulfillment in Christ

---

[22] Bergsma and Pitre, Kindle Location, 15914.

[23] Bergsma and Pitre, Kindle Location, 15914.

[24] Bergsma and Pitre, Kindle Location, 16399. The seven times *alma* is used in the Old Testament are Genesis 24:43; Exodus 2:8; Psalm 68:25; Proverbs 30:19; Songs 1:3; Songs 6:8; and Isaiah 7:14.

[25] Pitre, 55.

and Mary. Since God is the primary author of Sacred Scripture the primary and ultimate way that the Emmanuel child and the virgin are fulfilled are in Christ and Mary.

However, points out Pitre, this does not mean that there may be preliminary fulfillments before the fulfillment in Christ. In a preliminary sense, the prophecy may be referring to a future son of Isaiah by a prophetess whom Isaiah refers to in the following chapter (Isaiah 8:3), or it may be referring to the son of Ahaz and his bride Abijah (2 Chron 29:1), who gave birth to King Hezekiah. As a righteous king, Hezekiah helped to save his people's unique identity by instituting religious reforms centered on true worship of God. The second book of Kings praises Hezekiah so much that it even states, "He trusted in the LORD the God of Israel; so that there was none like him among all the kings of Judah after him, nor among all the kings who were before him (2 Kings 18:5 *RSVCE*)."

The Gospel of Matthew interprets the Immanuel child and the virgin as fulfilled ultimately in Christ who is God among us by the Incarnation and who surpasses King Hezekiah in righteousness as the divine King of the Universe.[26]

Chapters 13-27 Oracles of Warning and Salvation

In this section, beginning with a condemnation of Babylon, Isaiah issues a series of warnings of divine judgment that also includes words of comfort and words of a time of salvation when after God has struck the wicked down the "whole earth … [will be] at rest and quiet" and

---

[26] Brant Pitre, 55-56; Bergsma and Pitre, Kindle Location, 16422.

people will "break forth into singing (Isaiah 14:7 *RSVCE*)."[27] During this time of salvation, justice and peace will reign.

Among the reasons given for the collapse of worldly power is idolatry, and the over-reliance on worldly power "protection of the [mighty Egyptian] Pharaoh (Isaiah 30:2 *RSVCE*)" and material resources, those contained in the storage room of King Solomon called

---

[27] Bergsma and Pitre, Kindle Location, 15936. Bergsma and Pitre comment, "Notice here that the oracles against the nations *begin with Babylon*, which actually receives two oracles (Is 13, 21). This undermines the impression sometimes given that the first half of the book is focused only on Assyria (Is 1-39), while the second half is focused *only* on Babylon (Is 40-66)."

[28] James Tissot [Public domain], "Isaiah, c. 1896-1902," https://commons.wikimedia.org/wiki/File:Tissot_Isaiah.jpg

"the House of the Forest (Isaiah 22:8 *RSVCE*; cf. 1 Kings 7:2; 1 Kings 10:17)." Such reliance on worldly resources and upon the powerful of the world is folly since God desires trust in Him over trust in our strength (Isaiah 30:15 *RSVCE*). When God called people to stop relying on worldly power represented by strong, fast horses (Isaiah 30:16) and instead to repent, "to weeping and mourning, to baldness and putting on of sackcloth" they either did not hear the call or refused to hear it since the response was not one of sorrow for sin and repentance but, bemoans Isaiah, "joy and gladness, slaying oxen and killing sheep, eating flesh and drinking wine" along with the attitude of "Let us eat and drink for tomorrow we die (Isaiah 22:13 *RSVCE*)."

Even though right after this verse Isaiah writes, "'Surely this iniquity will not be forgiven you till you die,' says the Lord God of hosts (Isaiah 22:14 *RSVCE*)" a few chapters later Isaiah praises God for a time of salvation and life that will follow the time of judgment and death. The "LORD of hosts" writes Isaiah, "will make for all peoples a feast of fat things, a feast of choice wines ... And he will destroy ... the covering that is cast over all peoples, the veil that is spread over all nations. He will swallow up death for ever, and the Lord God will wipe away tears from all faces, and the reproach of his people he will take away from all the earth (Isaiah 25:6-8 *RSVCE*)."

During these this time of life when "the desert shall rejoice and blossom (Isaiah 35:1 *RSVCE*) ... the deaf shall hear ... the eyes of the blind shall see (Isaiah 29:17-18 *RSVCE*)." In reference to these signs of restoration, Jesus affirmed his identity as the divinely sent savior by responding to disciples of John the Baptist who asked Him, "Are you he who is to come, or shall we look for another (Matthew 11:3 *RSVCE*)?" with "Go and tell John what you hear and see: the blind receive their sight and the lame walk, lepers are cleansed and the deaf hear, and the dead are raised up, and the poor have good new preached to them (Matthew 11:5 *RSVCE*)."

Similarly, Luke's gospel describes Jesus as observing the sabbath by attending a synagogue service "as was his custom." When invited to read from the bible, Jesus turned to the passage in Isaiah which describes an anointed one who will "preach good new to the poor...release to the captives" and restore "sight to the blind." After closing the Bible, Jesus sat down and boldly revealed his Messianic identity by saying, "Today this Scripture has been fulfilled in your hearing (Matthew 4:18-21 *RSVCE*)." In so doing, Jesus also revealed himself as the teacher whom Isaiah prophecies will one day come. According to Isaiah, there will come a day when, "your Teacher will not hide himself anymore, but your eyes shall see your Teacher. And your ears shall hear a word behind you, saying 'This is the way, walk in it' (Isaiah 30:20-21 *RSVCE*)." Jesus is not only the voice who points us to the way but also is "the way, the truth and the life (John 14:6 *RSVCE*)."

The first section of Isaiah ends with King Hezekiah who as a righteous savior king prepared for the coming of Jesus the one perfectly righteous king. In chapter thirty-nine, Hezekiah demonstrates his imperfectness, his weakness by welcoming the envoys of the powerful king of Babylon by showing "them his treasure, house, the silver, the gold, the spices, the precious oil, his whole armory, all that was found in his storehouses. There was nothing in his house or in all his realm that Hezekiah did not show them (Isaiah 39:2 *RSVCE*)."

Isaiah confronts Hezekiah's proud indiscretion by telling Hezekiah, "Behold, the days are coming, when all that is in your house, and that which your fathers have stored up till this day, shall be carried to Babylon; nothing shall be left, says the Lord (Isaiah 39:5 *RSVCE*)." Instead of maintaining his trust in God, Hezekiah chose to act like his father Ahaz who aligned himself with the powerful Assyrian Empire rather than being faithful to God. In demonstration of how much he was willing to submit to the King of Assyria, Ahaz even "shut the doors of the house of the LORD [the Jerusalem Temple] and he made himself altars in every corner of Jerusalem. In every city of Judah, he made

---

[29] James Tissot [Public domain], "Brooklyn Museum – He Heals the Lame (Il guérit les boiteux)," https://commons.wikimedia.org/wiki/File:Brooklyn_Museum_-_He_Heals_the_Lame_(Il_gu%C3%A9rit_les_ boiteux)_-_James_Tissot.jpg.

high places to burn incense to other gods, provoking to anger the Lord, the God of this fathers (2 Chronicles 28:24-25 *RSVCE*)."

The very powers that Ahaz and Hezekiah trusted over God were great enemies of God's chosen people. The Assyrians in 722 B.C. defeated and deported the Kingdom of Israel, and the Babylonians defeated and deported the Kingdom of Judah in 586 B.C.

Section Questions

1. Why does Isaiah condemn liturgical practice and how is this similar to how Jesus corrects some Pharisees and John teaching in 1 John 4:20?

2. How is Isaiah purified in chapter six?

3. How can the Immanuel Child be fulfilled in 7:14 both in the Old Testament and in the New Testament?

4. "For the yoke of his burden, and the staff for his shoulder, the rod of his oppressor, thou hast broken as on the day of Mid'ian (Isaiah 9:4)." How does Justin Martyr interpret this passage and how is this interpretation justified if the writer of Isaiah did not intend this meaning? Include in your response the following: Primary Author, Secondary Author, Surplus of Meaning.

5. What are specific characteristics of the future kingdom that the messianic child will begin? Include in your answer the following: Peace, Weapons of War, Remnant, Nations, Exodus.

6. According to Isaiah what are the characteristics which will follow the time of judgment and death?

7. How does Hezekiah imperfectly foreshadow Jesus? In your response include the following: Babylonians, Trust, Saving King.

Isaiah Part II Section One Chapters 40—55: Hope and Consolation

Section one of Isaiah Part II focuses on the return home from Babylonian captivity of the people from the Southern Kingdom of

---

[30] Illustrations by E. M. Lilien (1874-1925) [Public domain], "Ephraim Moses Lilien, Zion, 1903," https://commons.wikimedia.org/wiki/File:Lieder_des_Ghetto_11.jpg.

Judah.[31] Unlike Part I of Isaiah that includes many messages of impending judgment and punishment this section contain messages of mercy, hope and consolation.[32] The first verse begins on a note of mercy with, "Comfort, comfort my people, say your God. Speak tenderly to Jerusalem, and cry to her that her warfare is ended, that her iniquity is pardoned, that she has received from the Lord's hand double for all her sins (Isaiah 40:1 *RSVCE*)." This is followed by verses that John the Baptist quotes, "The voice of one crying in the wilderness: Prepare the way of the Lord, make his paths straight (Matthew 3:3 *RSVCE*; cf. Isaiah 40:3)." The Lord who has come in the flesh is Jesus Christ who incarnationally shows forth the merciful, comforting countenance of God.

The following chapter contains the first of seven so called servant songs. From the perspective of the human author who wrote Isaiah, the suffering servant may refer, explains Bergsma and Pitre, to a Messiah, to Israel as a whole, to Isaiah, to the prophet Jeremiah, to Moses, or to an unknown person.[33] Bergsma and Pitre argue that the various proposed identities for the servant are not mutually exclusive of one another. The text at times indicates that the servant is an individual and at other times all of Israel, "But you, Israel, my servant (Isaiah 41:8 *RSVCE*)." Understood in this manner, comment Bergsma and Pitre:

> what happens to the individual servant of the Lord will also happen to the "servants of the Lord" collectively. Just as the

---

[31] McConville, 23.

[32] Bergsma and Pitre, Kindle Location, 16040.

[33] Bergsma and Pitre, Kindle Location, 16512.

individual servant suffered rejection, persecution, and death, followed by vindication, so too the servants of the Lord will go through tribulation and persecution but will ultimately be vindicated by God in the new heavens and the new earth.[34]

Catholic tradition interprets the servant reference of "Israel, my servant (Isaiah 41:8 *RSVCE*)" in chapter forty-one as ultimately fulfilled in Jesus who, "came not to be served to serve, and to give his life as a ransom for many (Matthew 20:28 *RSVCE*)." By extension, through Christ, the servant also applies to all the baptized, for the baptized are incorporated into the one body of Christ in whom all are to think with the mind of Jesus and love with the heart of Jesus (1 Corinthians 12:12-31 *RSVCE*).

As the perfect servant Jesus was rejected, persecuted, and killed, genuine servants of the Lord will also experience the same treatment in this world, but always with the hope to be saved by God who will one day perfectly renew all of creation. The suffering, rejection and death experienced by servants of God are intended to have a restorative purpose, and the suffering will if the servants are united to the life of the perfect servant, Jesus Christ. For this reason, the servant in Isaiah that Jesus fulfills, comment Bergsma and Pitre, "embodies Israel yet has a mission to restore Israel and call the nations to the Lord as well."[35]

Jesus' giving his life as a ransom reached its apex as he lay dying on the Cross. On the Cross, Jesus perfectly fulfilled the suffering servant of Isaiah, "He was despised and rejected by men; a man of

---

[34] Bergsma and Pitre, Kindle Location, 16550.

[35] Bergsma and Pitre, Kindle Location, 16140.

sorrows and acquainted with grief…. Surely, he has born our griefs and carried our sorrows (Isaiah 53:3-4 *RSVCE*)." Matthew applies this verse of Isaiah to Jesus as he healed people possessed by demons:

> That evening they brought to him many who were possessed with demons; and he cast out the spirits with a word and healed all who were sick. This was to fulfil what was spoken by the prophet Isaiah, "He took our infirmities and bore our diseases." (Matthew 8:16-17 *RSVCE*)

Similarly, Philip in Acts, tells an Ethiopian Eunuch who was reading Isaiah that Jesus fulfills the verses that immediately follow the verses we are reflecting upon, "like a lamb that is led to the slaughter and like a sheep that before its shearers is silent so he opened not his mouth (Isaiah 53:7; Acts 8:32 *RSVCE*)." in a teaching on suffering injustice patiently and quietly, St. Peter also refers to these verses of Isaiah, "But if when you do right and suffer for it you take it patiently, you have God's approval. For to this you have been called, because Christ also suffered for you, leaving you an example, that you should follow in his steps. He committed no sin; no guile was found on his lips. When he was reviled, he did not revile in return; when he suffered, he did not threaten; but he trusted to him who judges justly (1 Peter 2:20-23 *RSVCE*)."

In the midst of the servant songs, Isaiah, praises a Persian King Cyrus by even calling him "anointed (Isaiah 45:1 *RSVCE*)" by God. In Hebrew the word anointed is *Mashiach* (מָשִׁיחַ), which translates into Messiah. Cyrus, a Messiah, prophecies Isaiah, will fulfill the role as a shepherd who saves "Israel…my [God's] servant …. Thus, says the

Lord, your Redeemer…. who says of Cyrus, 'He is my shepherd (Isaiah 44:21, 24, 28 *RSVCE*)." In commenting on this passage, Benedict XVI writes that Isaiah:

> does not disdain to call Cyrus God's "anointed." The king of the Persians, who does not know the God of Israel and who is prompted by purely pragmatic political considerations when he sends the people back to their native land, is acting as God's instrument, since he is endeavoring to establish the correct state of affairs.

In continuity with this Old Testament understanding of God working through authority, including non-Israelite authority, Jesus, continues Benedict XVI:

> answers the Pharisees and the Herodians when they pose the controversial question of paying taxes: "Render to Caesar the things that are Caesar's" (Mark 12:13-17). Since the Roman emperor is the guarantor of law, he has a claim to obedience, though of course Jesus at once specifies the boundaries of the sphere in which one is obliged to obey: there are things that belong to Caesar and things that belong to God. If the emperor exalts himself to a divine position, he has gone beyond his proper limits, and obedience would then amount to a denial of God. Finally, Jesus' reply to Pilate belongs here too. The Lord acknowledges in his words to this unjust judge that the authority to exercise the judicial office, which is at the service

of the law, can be bestowed only from above (John 19:11).[36]

The fifth servant song (Isaiah 49:1-13) prophecies of a servant whose mission Jesus fulfills by offering salvation to all: "I will give you as a light to the nations, that my salvation may reach to the end of the earth (Isaiah 49:6 *RSVCE*)." This servant will "bring Jacob back to him, and that Israel might be gathered to him (Isaiah 49:5 RSVCE)." Responding to some who identify the servant with Israel, Miller asks: "How can Israel redeem Israel? How can Israel imagined as a character redeem a remnant of Israel?"[37] The Christian answer is the servant is not Israel but rather Jesus who offers redemption to the Israel of old and to the new Israel. Jesus explicitly identifies himself with this servant: "I am the light of the world; he who follows me will not walk in darkness, but will have the light of life (John 8:12 *RSVCE*)." This same servant song also identifies the servant as not only a "light" but also a covenant in person: "I have kept you and given you as a covenant to the people (Isaiah 49:8 *RSVCE*)." As pointed out by Bergsma and Pitre, the context in which this new covenant will be established is a meal:[38]

> Ho, everyone who thirsts, come to the waters; and he who has no money, come, buy and eat! Come, buy wine and milk without money and without price. Why do you spend your

---

[36] Joseph Ratzinger, *Values in a Time of Upheaval: Meeting the Challenges of the Future*, trans. Brian McNeil (San Francisco: Ignatius Press, 2006), Kindle location, 169 of 2245.

[37] Miller, 261.

[38] Bergsma and Pitre, Kindle Location, 16491.

money for that which is not bread, and your labor for that which does not satisfy? Hearken diligently to me, and eat what is good, and delight yourselves in fatness. Incline your ear, and come to me; hear, that your soul may live; and I will make with you an everlasting covenant, my steadfast, sure love for David (Isaiah 55:1-3 *RSVCE*).

In fulfillment of this promise, Jesus refers to himself as the new covenant when instituting the sacred meal of the Eucharist. Luke records that as he took the cup he said, "This cup which is poured out for you is the new covenant in my blood (Luke 22:20 *RSVCE*)."

Jesus's poured out his blood along with water when his side was pierced by a soldier's spear shortly after Jesus died on the cross (John 19:34). The blood and water have traditionally been interpreted as a sign that Jesus poured out his presence in two primary ways: through the Sacraments of the Eucharist and Baptism. Through these two sacraments, as with all sacraments, Jesus extends his presence in time by means of his Mystical Body, the Church.

Isaiah's sixth (Isaiah 50:4-11) and seventh servant songs (Isaiah 52:13-53:12) have also been traditionally interpreted in reference to Jesus' pouring out of himself in his passion: "I gave my back to those who struck me, and my cheeks to those who pulled out the beard; I hid not my face from shame and spitting (Isaiah 50:6 *RSVCE*)"; "Behold, my servant shall prosper, he shall be exalted and lifted up, and shall be very high. As many were astonished at him his appearance was so marred, beyond human semblance (Isaiah 52:13-114 *RSVCE*)." This song also identifies the servant as sinless: "The Lord God has opened my ear, and I was not rebellious, I turned not backward (Isaiah 50:5

RSVCE)." "And they made his grave with the wicked and with a rich man in his death, although he had done no violence, and there was no deceit in his mouth (Isaiah 53:9 *RSVCE*)." As sinless, Christianity believes that Jesus fulfills this prophecy as well by offering redemption to Israel, which the song, observes Miller, describes as sinful and in need of redemption (Isaiah 50:1-2).[39]

Despite being treated so, the servant does not despair but trusts in God: "For the Lord God helps me; therefore I have not been confounded; therefore I have set my face like a flint, and I know that I shall not be put to shame; he who vindicates me is near (Isaiah 50:7 *RSVCE*)." As the suffering servant, Jesus is vindicated by His resurrection from the dead, proof that truthful love is more powerful than hatred, than violence, than sin, than disordered love. By His resurrection Jesus's passion was transformed into a form of healing for the human dimension of his Mystical Body, so wounded by sin accumulated through centuries of disordered love: "…upon him was the chastisement that made us whole, and with his stripes we are healed (Isaiah 53:5 *RSVCE*).

Section Questions

1. The servant in the Servant songs can refer to the following: Messiah, Israel, Isaiah, Jeremiah, Moses, Unknown Person. Explain why these references are not mutually exclusive to one another.
2. What title is King Cyrus given in Isaiah 45:1 and why?

---

[39] Miller, 261.

Isaiah Part II Section Two Chapters 56-66: New Creation

Part two, section two contain prophecies of a time where all of creation, as a "macro-temple," Jerusalem and its holy Temple will be renewed. This promise of a new creation by Isaiah (Isaiah 65:17, 66:12) is brought to fulfillment by Christ's passion and resurrection. His redeeming passion, by way of application, is completed in time through His Church.[40] As Paul states, "in my flesh I complete what is lacking in Christ's afflictions for the sake of his body, that is, the church Col 1:24 *RSVCE*)." Paul also writes that, "if anyone is in Christ, he is a new creation; the old has passed away, behold, the new has come (2 Corinthians 5:17 *RSVCE*)." The new creation comes about by participating in the birth pangs of Christ's passion which leads to sharing in His resurrection. Building upon the Old Testament understanding of the entire universe, writes Bergsma and Pitre, the created universe is properly understood as a "macro-temple" and the temple as a "microcosm". Christ as the new Temple that after being destroyed is raised in three days (John 2:19) renews all of creation the "macro-temple" that was created to worship God.[41] As the *Catechism of the Catholic Church* teaches, "The visible universe, then, is itself destined to be transformed, 'so that the world itself, restored to its

---

[40] Dawn Eden Goldstein, *The Mystical Body and its Loving Wounds: Redemptive Suffering in Magisterial Teaching* (Mundelein: Doctoral Dissertation, 2016), 37. Here Dr. Goldstein distinguishes between "objective and subjective redemption" while referencing Pius XII's *Mystici corporis*, and Walter Kasper, *Jesus the Christ: New Edition* (London: T&T Clark, 2011), 192.

[41] Bergsma and Pitre, Kindle Location, 16478.

original state, facing no further obstacles, should be at the service of the just,' sharing their glorification in the risen Jesus Christ (*CCC* 1047)."[42]

In its renewed state, creation, Jerusalem, and the temple will be a "house of prayer for all peoples (Isaiah 56:7 *RSVCE*)." After firmly cleansing the Jerusalem Temple by overturning money-changers' tables, Jesus quoted this verse of Isaiah (Matthew 21:12-13 *RSVCE*). In so doing, Jesus was anticipating the time when there will be a new Temple open to all people. The new Temple is Jesus' body and by extension his mystical presence in the Catholic Church through which all are invited to participate in Jesus' body (1 Corinthians 12:12-31). Jesus explicitly identifies himself with the Messiah, the anointed one, who will "bring good tidings to the afflicted" by proclaiming "liberty to captives… opening of the prison to those who are bound (Isaiah 61:1 *RSVCE*)." Similarly, Jesus says to the disciples of John the Baptist, "Go and tell John what you hear and see: the blind receive their sight and the lame walk, lepers are cleansed and the deaf hear, and the dead are raised up, and the poor have good news preached to them (Matthew 11:4-5 *RSVCE*)."

Although all are invited to be part of this redeeming transformation, Isaiah prophecies that some will not accept this universally offered gift. Respecting this mystery of human freedom, God speaking through Isaiah proclaims that the redeemed "shall go forth and look on the dead bodies of the men that have rebelled against me; for their worm shall not die, their fire shall not be quenched, and

---

[42] "Catechism of the Catholic Church," vatican.va, http://www.vatican.va/archive/ccc_css/archive/catechism/p123a12.htm#VI, no. 1047.

they shall be an abhorrence to all flesh (Isaiah 66:24 *RSVCE*)." God will, though, "marry" those who do accept the Good News of salvation. Even the land where this marriage will take place will be married: "...you shall be called My delight is in her, and your land Married; for the Lord delights in you, and your land shall be married (Isaiah 62:4 *RSVCE*)." In this marriage between God and creation the two will "become one flesh (Genesis 2:24 *RSVCE*)."

This transforming union was fulfilled at the Incarnation when Jesus took on human flesh while fully retaining his divine nature, for both his humanity and divinity were united in His one Divine Person. Mary's painless birth of the union of divinity and humanity in the one person of Jesus Christ is prophesied, according to Church Fathers, in the last chapter of Isaiah: "Before she was in labor, she gave birth; before her pain came upon her she was delivered of a son. Who has heard of such a thing? (Isaiah 66:7-8 *RSVCE*)"[43] In commenting on these verses, the Church Father Methodius of Olympus writes:

> The most holy virgin mother, therefore, escaped entirely the manner of women even before she gave birth, doubtless in order that with the Holy Spirit betrothing her to himself and sanctifying her, she might conceive without intercourse with man. She has brought forth her firstborn Son, even the only-begotten Son of God . . . who on earth, in the Virgin's nuptial chamber, joined to himself the nature of Adam, like a bridegroom, by an inalienable union, and he preserved his mother's purity incorrupt and uninjured; him in short who in heaven was begotten without corruption and on earth birthed

---

[43] Bergsma and Pitre, Kindle Location, 16634.

in a manner quite unspeakable.[44]

As the perfect priest who ushers in the new creation by acting as a bridge and one mediator between creation and the creator, Jesus transforms the exclusive Levitical priesthood into a priesthood that all can participate in, in various degrees and kinds. This universal priesthood, grounded in Christ, observe Bergsma and Pitre, is also prophesied by Isaiah when in the concluding chapter he describes God as taking "some of them [the Gentiles] ... for priests and for Levites (Isaiah 66:21 *RSVCE*)"

Section Questions

1. How is the new creation prophesied in Isaiah fulfilled by Jesus and the Catholic Church? Include the following in your response: Temple, Microcosm, Macro-temple, *Catechism of the Catholic Church*.
2. How is Isaiah's prophecy that "your land shall be married (Isaiah 62:4)" spiritually fulfilled by Jesus along with Mary?

---

[44] Mark W. Elliott, *Ancient Christian Commentary on Scripture; Old Testament XI, Isaiah 40-66* (Downers Grove: InterVarsity Press, 2007), 354; "The deepening of faith in the virginal motherhood led the Church to confess Mary's real and perpetual virginity even in the act of giving birth to the Son of God made man. In fact, Christ's birth 'did not diminish his mother's virginal integrity but sanctified it.' And so the liturgy of the Church celebrates Mary as *Aeiparthenos*, the 'Ever-virgin'." "Catechism of the Catholic Church," vatican.va, http://www.vatican.va/archive/ccc_css/archive/catechism/p122a3p2.htm, no. 499.

Jeremiah

Introduction

The first verse of Jeremiah identifies him as "the son of Hilkiah," and a priest from Anathoth from the southern Kingdom of Judah, specifically from the "land of Benjamin (Jeremiah 1:1 *RSVCE*)." Jeremiah's name in Hebrew is *Yirmeyah* (יִרְמְיָה), meaning God (*yah*) loosens.[1] According to Bergsma and Pitre, in the context of the book, Jeremiah's name means that God will loosen by restoring.[2] Chapter thirty-two describes this restoration as consisting of God gathering the Israelites, especially those scattered in various countries of the world, back to the Promised Land: "Behold, I will gather them from all the countries to which I drove them in my anger and my wrath … I will bring them back to this place, and I will them dwell in safety (Jeremiah 32:37 *RSVCE*)."

Jeremiah witnessed a further scattering of his people. The first major scattering happened a number of centuries before Jeremiah in 722 when the Assyrian Empire defeated and deported the northern Kingdom of Israel. Then, during Jeremiah's lifetime, in 586 B.C. the Babylonian Empire defeated the southern Kingdom of Judah and similarly deported its people. Jeremiah was not one of those who were deported. Instead, he was left behind along with other people the Babylonians did not deem as a threat. The people

---

[1] "3414. Yirmeyah or Yirmeyahu," biblehub.com, https://biblehub.com/hebrew/3414.htm.

[2] John Bergsma and Brant Pitre, *A Catholic Introduction to the Bible, Volume I* (San Francisco: Ignatius Press, 2018), Kindle Location, 16786.

who remained fled to Egypt, forcefully taking Jeremiah and Baruch with them (Jeremiah 43:1-7). In protest, Jeremiah warned, "O remnant of Judah, 'Do not go to Egypt.' Know for a certainty that I have warned you this day....
...know for certainty that you shall die by the sword, by famine, and by pestilence in the place where you desire to go to live (Jeremiah 42:19, 22 *RSVCE*)."

Prior to the Babylonian conquest of Judah, Jeremiah lived through the reigns of a number of kings. Those mentioned in the first chapter are Josiah, Jehoiakim, and Zedekiah. Missing from this list is Jehoahaz who reigned three months in 609 B.C. between the reigns of Josiah and Jehoiakim and Jehoiachin who reigned between Jehoiakim and Zedekiah. The complete list of succession from c. 640 to c. 586 B.C. is as follows: Josiah, Jehoahaz, Jehoiakim, Jehoiachin, and Zedekiah.

Under King Josiah's reign the "the book of the law (2 Kings 22:8)" was found by the high priest Hilkiah the High priest. Upon hearing the words of the book, which mandated fidelity to the Mosaic law, Hilkiah instituted a religious reform among his people, beginning with himself by bringing to an end the worship of false gods (2 Kings 22-23). Josiah was followed by his son King Jehoahaz (2 Chronicles 36:1). After only three months of reigning, Jehoahaz was deported by the Egyptian Pharaoh Neco who installed Jehoahaz's brother Eliakim king of Judah while giving Eliakim a new name, Jehoiakim (2 Chronicles 36:1-4 *RSVCE*). Jehoiakim switched his allegiance to the Babylonians when the Babylonians defeated the Egyptians who had allied themselves with Assyrian forces at the 605 B.C. Battle of Carchemish (Jeremiah 46:2).[3]

At first, Jehoiakim submitted to King Nebuchadnezzar's authority but then he decided to place his trust in Egyptian power, despite Jeremiah warning him not to. Jeremiah warned Jehoiakim by writing on a scroll, warnings and a call to repentance. Jehoiakim responded by ordering the

---

[3] Bergsma and Pitre, Kindle Location, 16818.

scroll to be read in his presence by a court official, Jehudi. As he listened, Jehoiakim cut of sections from the scroll and threw them into a fire until the entire scroll was burned (Jeremiah 36:20-25).

Stubbornly, Jehoiakim refused to repent and instead placed his trust in worldly power and adopted worldly ways by doing "evil in the sight of the Lord (2 Kings 23:37 *RSVCE*)." Providentially, God permitted Jehoiakim to be humbled when King Nebuchadnezzar deported many of people of Judah including Jehoiakim (2 Chronicles 36:6). Jehoiakim was in turn succeeded by his son Jehoiachin who imitated his father's evil, rebellious ways (2 Chronicles 36:9) and was also deported by King Nebuchadnezzar after only ruling "three months and ten days in Jerusalem (2 Chronicles 36:9 *RSVCE*)."

Nebuchadnezzar then established Jehoiakim's brother Zedekiah as king over Judah (2 Chronicles 36:5-10 *RSVCE*). Zedekiah ruled "eleven years in Jerusalem (2 Chronicles 36:11 *RSVCE*)." Like his brother and father, Zedekiah "did what was evil in the sight of the Lord (2 Kings 24:19 *RSVCE*)" rebelled against the Babylonians, sided with the Egyptians and was deported to Babylon along with his people. In Babylon, Zedekiah's sons where slain before him and Zedekiah's eyes were gouged out (Jeremiah 39:6-7 *RSVCE*). The Babylonians further humiliated the Jewish people by burning down Jerusalem, including the temple (Jeremiah 39:8, 52:13).

Gedaliah was then appointed by Nebuchadnezzar as governor of the remaining people in Jerusalem. Gedaliah was the son of Ahikam who protected Jeremiah when King Jehoiakim wanted to kill Jeremiah as Jehoiakim had killed the prophet Uriah the son of Shemaiah who "prophesied... in words like those of Jeremiah (Jeremiah 26:20 *RSVCE*)." As governor, Gedaliah told his people of Judah that they were to "serve the king of Babylon, and it shall be well for you (Jeremiah 40:9 *RSVCE*)." Hearing that Jerusalem had a Jewish governor who was approved by Nebuchadnezzar, Jewish people began to resettle in the land of Judah. God blessed those obediently gathered around Gedaliah and Jeremiah with "wine and summer fruits in great abundance (Jeremiah 40:12 RSVCE)." Sadly, though, Gedaliah was assassinated by the Israelite, Ishmael who, supported by a group of rebels, "slew all Jews who were with Gedaliah...and the Chaldean [Babylonian] soldiers who happened to be there (Jeremiah 41:3 *RSVCE*)."

Hearing of the evil that Ishmael had committed, Johanan son of Kareah led men in battle against Gedaliah. Ishmael and some of his followers escaped to the land of the Ammonites. In fear of retaliation by the Babylonians, Johanan wanted to lead his people to Egypt, far away from the Babylonians. When Jeremiah was consulted, Jeremiah insisted that they remain in the land of Judah, are not to fear the Babylonians and their king, and are trust in God instead of trusting in the power of the Egyptians (Jeremiah 42). Ignoring Jeremiah, Johanan led the people living in the land of Judah to Egypt. Jeremiah and Baruch were forced to accompany this disobedient flight to Egypt (Jeremiah 43). In Egypt, Jeremiah continued to prophecy to his people warning them that "that none of the remnant of Judah who have come to live in the land of Egypt shall escape or survive or return to the land of Judah (Jeremiah 44:14 *RSVCE*)." According to an ancient tradition that Jerome refers to, the Judean people responded to Jeremiah's prophecy by stoning him to death.[4]

We will not look at the various sections of Jeremiah, following the divisions of David A. Dorsey.[5]

Section Questions

1. What does Jeremiah's name, *Yirmeyah* (יִרְמְיָה) mean?

---

[4] Dean O. Wenthe, *Ancient Christian Commentary on Scripture: Old Testament XII Jeremiah, Lamentations*, (Downers Grove, InterVarsity Press, 2009), 59. Jerome's *Against Jovinianus*, 2.37 is cited.

[5] Barclay M. Newman and Philip C. Stine, *A Handbook on Jeremiah* (New York: United Bible Societies, 2003), 1.; David A. Dorsey, *The Literary Structure of the Old Testament* (Grand Rapids: Baker Academic, 1999), 244.

2. Of the following names which one was not a king of Judah, and what was he instead? Josiah, Jehoahaz, Gedaliah, Jehoiakim, Jehoiachin, and Zedekiah

Punishment of Judah (1:1-12:17) [6]

The first chapter opens by briefly introducing Jeremiah which is followed by God commissioning him with, "Before I formed you in the womb I knew you, and before you were born I consecrated you; I appointed you a prophet to the nations ... to pluck up and to break down, to destroy and to overthrow, to build and to plant (Jeremiah 1:5, 10 *RSVCE*)." Bergsma and Pitre observe that these verses well describe the tone of Jeremiah's prophecy. Although Jeremiah does intersperse his prophetic message with positive, hopeful messages, indicated by the last two verbs "to build and to plant" he emphasizes divine judgement more as the first four verbs indicate, "to pluck up and to break down, to destroy and to overthrow."[7]

A specific practice that Jeremiah immediately identifies as actions that God will overthrow are liturgical practices that include worship to false Gods (Jeremiah 1:16). Later in chapter seven, point out Bergsma and Pitre, Jeremiah describes abhorrent false worship where "the sons of Judah...burn their sons and daughters in the fire" something that "I [God] did not command, nor did it come to my mind (Jeremiah 7:31 *RSVCE*)." What God does command, preaches Jeremiah, is upright worship by which people do not work on the Sabbath day since they are intent on keeping the Sabbath holy (Jeremiah 17:24).

When this occurs, people will be drawn to the true worship "from the cities of Judah and the places round about Jerusalem ... bringing burnt offerings and sacrifices, cereal offerings and frankincense, and bringing

---

[6] Newman and Stine, 244.

[7] Bergsma and Pitre, Kindle Location, 16929.

thank offerings to the house of the Lord (Jeremiah 17:26 *RSVCE*)." This passage and others, argue Bergsma and Pitre, clearly indicate that Jeremiah is not preaching that liturgical worship it itself is wrong. Rather, he is preaching that false worship displeases God, and true worship pleases God. In true worship, the worshiper's actions both outside of the worship and within the worship correspond to the holiness of God.[8]

Jeremiah's repeated rejection by his people anticipates Jesus' rejection right from the time he was a baby. When the baby Jesus was presented in the Temple by Mary and Joseph, Simeon prophesied that Jesus would cause division in order to lay bare the hearts of many, some of whom would repent and rise in the life of Christ: "Behold, this child is set for the fall and rising of many in Israel, and for a sign that is spoken against… that thoughts of many hearts may be revealed (Luke 2:34-35 *RSVCE*)."

Chapters two through six compares Jerusalem to an unfaithful bride married to God. This bride refuses to admit her guilt of infidelity by idolatry coupled with injustice to the "guiltless poor (Jeremiah 2:34 *RSVCE*)." In response God warns, "Behold, I will bring you to judgment for saying, 'I have not sinned (Jeremiah 2:35 *RSVCE*)." In the midst of these prophecies of judgment, comments Bergsma and Pitre, there is hope for forgiveness, hope that was not present in human marriages of that time. Jeremiah rhetorically asks, "If a man divorces his wife and she goes from him and becomes another man's wife, will he return to her? (Jeremiah 3:1 *RSVCE*)" The answer is no. However, Jeremiah adds, since God's ways are not man's ways God will not look at his faithless bride Israel "in anger, for I am merciful (Jeremiah 3:12 *RSVCE*)." In the following chapter, God, through Jeremiah, beseeches Israel to "return (Jeremiah 4:1 *RSVCE*)."

Chapters seven through nine warn of punishment if Israel does not return, does not repent. In chapter seven, Israel is warned that simply worshipping in the Jerusalem Temple is not sufficient. This worship must

---

[8] Bergsma and Pitre, Kindle Location, 17297.

also be accompanied by keeping the Ten Commandments and by not worshipping false Gods outside of Temple worship. If worship in the Temple is not accompanied by a morally upright life and the rejection of idolatry then the Temple worship, no matter how holy it may appear to be, is worthless. In punishment, God will turn Jerusalem and her Holy Temple into "a heap of ruins (Jeremiah 9:11 *RSVCE*)."

This warning of punishment is followed by two chapters which condemns Israel's adultery by the worship of false gods and consequent breaking of the covenant of love with God. As long as the idolatry and breaking of the Ten Commandments continues then Israel's worship is rejected by God since it is hypocritical. "What right has my beloved in my house, when she has done vile deeds? Can vows and sacrificial flesh avert your doom? (Jeremiah 11:15 *RSVCE*)" This prophecy of punishment calls forth a response of hatred towards Jeremiah: "I was like a gentle lamb led to the slaughter. I did not know it was against me they devised schemes, saying, Let us destroy the tree with its fruit, let us cut him off from the land of the living, that his name be remembered no more (Jeremiah 11:19 *RSVCE*)." The people do not want to remember Jeremiah, and even his name since his words stirs their consciences. Bergsma and Pitre relate the reference of Jeremiah as a "gentle lamb led to the slaughter" by angry scheming people who are upset by Jeremiah's preaching of upright living to John the Baptist calling Jesus "the Lamb of God (John 1:29 *RSVCE*)." In fulfillment of Jeremiah's rejection, Jesus as a gentle lamb also will experience people plotting against Him with the desire to eliminate His presence so as not to be bothered by his words and blameless life.[9]

Section Questions

1. According to Jeremiah 3:1, how is God's fidelity unlike the fidelity

---

[9] Bergsma and Pitre, Kindle Location, 17353.

of men to unfaithful wives?

2. How do Jeremiah's words, "I was like a gentle lamb led to the slaughter" foreshadow Jesus' reception by this world? Include in your answer the following: John the Baptist.

Divine Plans for Judah's Fall (13:1-20:18)[10]

In this section Jeremiah does a number of symbolic actions that point to God's plans for Judah to be humbled from her proud, disobedient, idolatrous ways. In chapter thirteen, Jeremiah is commanded by God to take the cloth Jeremiah wears wrapped around his loins and bury it in a crack of a rock. Days later, God tells Jeremiah to dig out the loin cloth, which has decayed and is useless. Like a loincloth that is to be wrapped intimately around its owner, the people of Judah are to remain intimately united in loyalty to God. Out of pride, the people have separated themselves from this intimate relationship and sought out false Gods. In separating themselves from God, they lost their value.

Jeremiah is also told in chapter thirteen to fill jars with wine. This action represents, explains God, that the people of Judah have become drunk with the pleasures of this world, lost their reason, and are acting in a self-destructive manner that God permits so as to heal them from their pride that has separated them from God.

Later, in chapter sixteen God commands Jeremiah not to marry and to deliberately be childless. Jeremiah's celibacy and consequent lack of physical fruitfulness is in tension with the divine commandment in the first chapter of Genesis to Adam and Eve to "be fruitful and multiply Genesis 1:28 *RSVCE*) since God is a God of life and not of death (Luke 20:38). Jeremiah's celibacy is to serve as a prophetic sign to the people of Judah of the diseases

---

[10] Newman and Stine, 1; David A. Dorsey, *The Literary Structure of the Old Testament* (Grand Rapids: Baker Academic, 1999), 244.

and death that awaits them for having refused to repent. The sign value of Jeremiah's celibacy is distinctly different from the celibacy and virginity of Catholics consecrated to God. In Catholicism, consecrated celibacy and virginity is not so much a sign of death but rather of eternal life and the possibility of, in participation in Christ's life, of spiritual fruitfulness by populating heaven with many people.

A few chapters later in chapter eighteen, Jeremiah obediently heeds the words of God he hears by visiting a potter working at his wheel. As he shapes a vessel out of clay the clay comes apart and he then reshapes the clay into a vessel. Similarly, explains God, Israel is in the hands of God who can reshape Israel into a pleasing form if Israel becomes deformed. The subsequent chapter likewise is on a vessel. This time Jeremiah is told to purchase a flask, and, after warning people of impending divine punishment, to "break the flask in the sight of the men (Jeremiah 19:10 *RSVCE*)" as a sign that God will break the people of Judah's proud ways for "they have stiffened their neck, refusing to hear my words (Jeremiah 19:15 *RSVCE*)."

Section Questions

1. What does Jeremiah's burial of his loincloth symbolize?
2. What does Jeremiah's filling jars with wine symbolize?
3. Contrast the practice of Catholic celibacy and virginity with Jeremiah's celibacy.
4. According to Jeremiah, what does the potter working at his wheel symbolize?

Divine Judgment and Punishment (21:1-29:32)[11]

Chapter twenty-one is addressed to King Zedekiah and the people of

---

[11] Newman and Stine, 1; Dorsey, 244.

Judah whom Jeremiah prophecies will be punished by God through the hands of the Babylonians: "I myself will fight against you.... I will give Zedekiah king of Judah ... and the people in this city ... into the hand of Nebuchadnezzar king of Babylon (Jeremiah 21:5-7 *RSVCE*)." This is followed by further promises of judgement and punishment in chapter twenty-two on kings of Judah who preceded Zedekiah: Jehoahaz (Shallum son of Josiah), and Jehoiachin (Coniah son of Jehoiakim). In condemning the abusive, unjust practices of Jehoahaz, Jeremiah laments Jehoahaz's vanity of building a "great house with spacious upper room...paneling it with cedar, and painting it with vermillion (Jeremiah 22:14 *RSVCE*)" while refusing to give wages to those who work for him. At the time, Miller comments, buildings in Judah were ordinarily made of limestone and not in wood since wood was exceedingly expensive to build with. Knowing this, Jehoahaz still imports cedar wood from Lebanon and proudly orders the cedar to be painted scarlet red.[12]

Chapter twenty-three then condemns wicked, "ungodly (Jeremiah 23:11 *RSVCE*)" prophets and priests. Regarding the wicked prophets God says, "I did not send the prophets, yet they ran; I did not speak to them, yet they prophesied (Jeremiah 23:21 *RSVCE*)." Jeremiah also prophecies that the people remaining in land of Judah will likewise be punished: "I will make them a horror to all the kingdoms of the earth, to be reproach, a byword, a taunt, and a curse in all the places where I shall drive them (Jeremiah 24:9 *RSVCE*)." Finally, Jeremiah prophecies that punishment awaits all people for God "is summoning a sword against all the inhabitants of the earth (Jeremiah 25:29 *RSVCE*)."

After preaching punishment for all people, Jeremiah prophecies that the holy Temple in Jerusalem will be destroyed along with the city: "I [God] will make this house like Shiloh, and I will make this city a curse for all the nations

---

[12] Robert D. Miller II, *Understanding the Old Testament* (Chantilly: The Teaching Company, 2019), 272.

of the earth (Jeremiah 26:6 *RSVCE*)." Hearing these words, the priests and members of the royal house of Judah tell the people of Judah that Jeremiah deserves to be executed. Ahikam saves Jeremiah from being killed at the hands of King Zedekiah who had killed another prophet who had prophesied in a similar manner to Jeremiah's prophecy.

In the following two chapters (26-27), Jeremiah once again is commanded by God to preach by doing a jarring, symbolic action. He makes a yoke, puts it around his neck and prophecies to the people of Judah that God has providentially allowed the king of Babylon, Nebuchadnezzar, to rule them. The people are to submit and obey this king as Jeremiah has submitted to wearing a yoke around his neck since this is the will of God for him. A false prophet, Hananiah, reacts by forcefully removing the yoke from Jeremiah's neck and breaking it while saying, "Thus says the LORD: Even so will I break the yoke of Nebuchadnezzar king of Babylon from the neck of all the nations within two years (Jeremiah 28:11 *RSVCE*)." Jeremiah tells Hananiah that "the Lord has not sent you, and you have made this people trust in a lie (Jeremiah 28:15 *RSVCE*)." He then prophecies that within that year, Hananiah will die for having preached falsehood that deceptively raised the people of Judah's hopes. The prophecy comes true and Hananiah dies.

The last chapter of this section contains Jeremiah's letter to the exiles living in Babylon. In the letter, Jeremiah counsels the people to patiently obey the king of Babylon while retaining belief that after seventy years of exile God will restore them back to their homeland. Jeremiah even tells the people to pray for their oppressors who are governing them: "...seek the welfare of the city where I have sent you into exile, and pray to the LORD on its behalf (Jeremiah 29:7 *RSVCE*)." Relating this passage to the New Testament, Benedict XVI writes:

> Although the Christians were being persecuted, they did not have a negative view of the state in principle, but, rather, they still recognized in it the state qua state and did what was in their power

to build it up as a state; they did not try to destroy it. Precisely because they knew that they were in "Babylon," they applied to themselves the guidelines that Jeremiah had written to the children of Israel who had been exiled to that place. The letter of the prophet that is recorded in chapter 29 of the Book of Jeremiah." ... We can read a very similar admonition in Paul's First Letter to Timothy, which tradition dates to the time of Nero, where it says to pray "for all men, for kings and all who are in high positions, that we may lead a quiet and peaceable life, godly and respectful in every way" (1 Tim 2:1-2)."[13]

Section Questions

1.   Why does Jeremiah insist that the Jewish people obey the Babylonian king and how does the yoke which Jeremiah places around his neck represent this? In addition, what does the false prophet Hananiah do to the yoke?

Restoration of Israel (30:1-33:26)[14]

A New Covenant is promised in this section: "I will make a new covenant with the house of Israel and the house of Judah ... I will put my law within the, and I will write it upon their hearts (Jeremiah 31:31, 33 *RSVCE*)." With these words, it is prophesied that one day the Northern Kingdom of Israel and its tribes which were scattered by the 722 B.C. Assyrian conquest will be gathered by the Lord and re-united with the Southern Kingdom of Judah.

---

[13] Benedict XVI, Joseph Ratzinger, *Faith and Politics Selected Writings*, trans. Michael J. Miller (San Francisco: Ignatius Press, 2018), Kindle Location, 988.

[14] Newman and Stine, 1; Dorsey, 244.

The Catholic Church believes that this prophecy is fulfilled in the Catholic Church, in the Mystical Body of Christ, in whom all are gathered as one new people of God whose covenant is the New Covenant in the person of Jesus, the perfect bridge between God and human beings. The New Law is living in the life of Jesus Christ along with all those who make up Jesus' Mystical Body.

Along with assuring that the Twelve Tribes will be re-united in a New Covenant, not in the sense of being brand new but renewed and perfected, Jeremiah also prophecies that the Davidic Kingship "shall never lack a man to sit on the throne of the house of Israel, and the Levitical priests shall never lack a man in my presence to offer burnt offerings, to burn cereal offerings [bread offerings], and to make sacrifices forever (Jeremiah 33:17 *RSVCE*)." Once again, this fidelity of God to his promises is fulfilled in Jesus Christ, as the eternal Davidic King who "sits" on a heavenly throne as king of the universe and who offered a perfect love sacrifice to his Heavenly Father on the cross. Every Mass that is celebrated in which bread and wine is offered and transformed into the body and blood of Jesus Christ participates in this perfect eternal of love that is true because it is eternal since God is the one who offered himself to reconcile us to Himself.

Interestingly, comment Bergsma and Pitre, an ancient *midrash* on Jewish Scripture interprets chapter thirty-three of Jeremiah as foretelling a time when the only sacrifice that will remain will be a thanksgiving sacrifice:

> Rabbi Pinchas, Rabbi Levi and Rabbi Yochanan [said] in the name of Rabbi Menachem from Gallia: **In the time to come, all sacrifices will be annulled - but the sacrifice of thanksgiving will not be annulled**. All prayers will be annulled, but **the prayer of gratitude will not be annulled**. This accords with what is written [Jeremiah 33:11]: "The voice of joy and the voice of gladness, the voice of the groom and the voice of the bride, the voice of those who say 'Give thanks to the LORD of hosts' etc." - this is the prayer of gratitude. "Those who bring [the sacrifice of] thanksgiving to the House of the

LORD": this is the sacrifice of thanksgiving. Thus David said: "I owe You vows and will offer you thanksgivings" [Psalms 56:13] - not "thanksgiving," but "thanksgivings," [indicating both] the thanksgiving prayer and the prayer of gratitude.[15]

The divine promise of the permanence of the Levitical priesthood is fulfilled in the sacrifice of thanksgiving of the Mass, of the Eucharist, which literally means in Greek thanksgiving. In explaining how the Levitical priesthood continues in the New Testament priesthood, Bergsma and Pitre write:

The early Church took the prophecies of the Old Testament seriously but, at the same time, saw them fulfilled both *Christologically* and *sacramentally*. It is no earthly throne or earthly priesthood that will constitute worship in the age of the Messiah, but the heavenly throne of Christ the King and the heavenly worship, in

---

[15] "Vayikra Rabbah," sefaria.org, https://www.sefaria.org/Vayikra_Rabbah.9.8?lang=bi, chapter 9. "Composed in Talmudic Israel/Babylon (500 CE). Vayikra Rabbah (The Great Leviticus) is a homiletic midrash to Leviticus. It is referred to by Nathan ben Jehiel (circa 1035–1106) and Rashi (1040–1105). It originated in the Land of Israel and is composed largely from older works. Its redactor made use of Genesis Rabbah, Pesikta de-Rav Kahana, and the Jerusalem and Babylonian Talmuds. It might have been written in 7th Century CE but others place it in the 5th Century. It is not a continuous explanatory interpretation to Leviticus, but a collection of exclusive sermons or lectures on the themes or texts of that book. It consists altogether of 37 such homilies, each of which constitutes a separate chapter. Leviticus Rabbah often refers to Scriptural passages on which the homilies are based as parashiyot and are further designated according to their content." Bergsma and Pitre, Kindle Location, 17321.

which the priests and deacons on earth participate whenever and wherever the Eucharist is celebrated. In other words, the temporal and earthly Levitical priesthood does not truly pass away with the coming of Christ; rather, it is perfected and fulfilled in the eternal and heavenly Melchizedekian priesthood of Christ in the new and everlasting covenant.

...

A key text is Acts 6:7, which records an important stage in the growth of the early Church: ... This text witnesses to the fact that a large number of the heirs of the Levitical covenant did, in fact, enter into the New Covenant. Did they lose their priestly status? No, for Peter testifies: ... (1 Pet 2:9). In the Church, every believer becomes a priest in Christ (*CCC* 901-3). The priesthood is not confiscated from the descendants of Levi but shared with the whole community. Therefore, the large number of Levitical priests who joined the New Covenant community in Acts 6:7 did not lose their priestly status, and in them and their descendants Jeremiah's words are fulfilled: "The Levitical priests shall never lack a man in my presence" (Jer 33:18).[16]

---

[16] Bergsma and Pitre, Kindle Location, 17417. **"The participation of lay people in Christ's priestly office** 901 'Hence the laity, dedicated as they are to Christ and anointed by the Holy Spirit, are marvelously called and prepared so that even richer fruits of the Spirit maybe produced in them. For all their works, prayers, and apostolic undertakings, family and married life, daily work, relaxation of mind and body, if they are accomplished in the Spirit - indeed even the hardships of life if patiently born - all these become spiritual sacrifices acceptable to God through Jesus Christ. In the celebration of the Eucharist these may most fittingly be offered to the Father along with the body of the Lord. and so, worshipping everywhere by their holy actions, the laity consecrate the world itself to God, everywhere offering worship by

Section Questions

1. How are the following prophesied by Jeremiah 31:31 fulfilled in the
    New Testament? New Covenant, New Law, Eternal Davidic
    Kingship, Eternal Sacrifice, Eternal Priesthood.

Jeremiah Preaching to Zedekiah and the Rechabites (34:1-35:19)[17]

Here, Jeremiah prophecies that King Zedekiah would die imprisoned in
Babylon for having refused to heed the Word of God spoken through
Jeremiah commanding Zedekiah to remain obedient to the Babylonian King
Nebuchadnezzar who had installed Zedekiah as king of Judah (2 Chronicles
36:5-10 *RSVCE*). God permitted Zedekiah to be humiliated in captivity
because, explains Jeremiah, Zedekiah had gone back on his word to follow
the commandment in Exodus to free Hebrew slaves after they has served for
six years (Exodus 21:2; Jeremiah 34:17 *RSVCE*). This commandment was
reinforced by Jeremiah's insistence as inspired by God "that everyone should
set free his Hebrew slaves, male and female, so that no one should enslave a

---

the holiness of their lives.' 902 In a very special way, parents share in the
office of sanctifying 'by leading a conjugal life in the Christian spirit and by
seeing to the Christian education of their children.' 903 Lay people who
possess the required qualities can be admitted permanently to the ministries
of lector and acolyte. When the necessity of the Church warrants it and when
ministers are lacking, lay persons, even if they are not lectors or acolytes, can
also supply for certain of their offices, namely, to exercise the ministry of the
word, to preside over liturgical prayers, to confer Baptism, and to distribute
Holy Communion in accord with the prescriptions of law.'" "Catechism of
the Catholic Church," vatican.va, http://www.vatican.va/archive/
ENG0015/_P2A.HTM.

[17] Newman and Stine, 1; Dorsey, 244.

Jew, his brother (Jeremiah 34:9 *RSVCE*)."

Zedekiah's condemnation is followed by Jeremiah praising the Rechabites (chapter 35). The Rechabites were descendants of Rechab (1 Chronicles 2:55), a Kenite. The Kenites were a non-Israelite tribe. Some of the Kenites, such as Moses's father in law joined the Israelites and were assimilated by the tribe of Judah (Judges 1:16). Even though the Israelites, and Judah as a tribe of Israel, were called by God to be an example for all nations to follow, to be a sign of fidelity to God, Judah, and through Judah, Israel, broke her promise of fidelity to God while the Rechabites, descendants of a pagan people, remained faithful to the true God they came to know and worship by their encounter with the Israel, with Judah.

Sometimes, people are called to repentance, are called to love truthfully by others who later become corrupted, who trade false, destructive, selfish love for true, social, other-centered love as formed by the Ten Commandment. The behavior of the fallen may cause those who received a message of repentance from them to become scandalized. The scandal, though, can be transformed into a steppingstone where the bad behavior serves as a reminder that God chooses to work through imperfect people in this world and God is the reason for the repentance and the ultimate reason to remain faithful. In addition, the scandal offers a providential opportunity to bring the gift of faithful love back to those whom we first received it from and who have fallen.

Section Questions

1. Why were the Rechabites praised and what was the ethnicity of their tribe?

Rejection of Jeremiah (36:1-45:5)[18]

Chapter thirty-six refers to a king, Jehoiakim, who preceded King Zedekiah. As stated previously, Jehoiakim spurned the reading of Jeremiah's prophetic scroll which warned the king to continue to submit to the Babylonian King while trusting that God one day will deliver them the Jewish people from oppression. To demonstrate his rejection of the scroll, Jehoiakim burned it bit by bit.

Jehoiakim's reign was followed by his son Jehoiachin who followed his father's rebellious ways and was forcefully removed from power by King Nebuchadnezzar. Nebuchadnezzar then appointed Zedekiah, Jehoiakim's brother, to rule over Judah (2 Chronicles 36:5-10 *RSVCE*).

In chapter thirty-seven, Jeremiah is imprisoned during Zedekiah's rule. In fear that Jeremiah's prophecy may come true, Zedekiah summons Jeremiah to question him. He then heeds Jeremiah's request not to return to prison and instead orders Jeremiah to be remain in "the court of the guard (Jeremiah 37:21 *RSVCE*).

Zedekiah's relatively benevolent attitude to Jeremiah changes when princes complain to Zedekiah that Jeremiah should be killed since he is discouraging the people, in particular the military, from defending the city from the Babylonians and instead telling them to surrender and cooperate with their conquerors. Zedekiah responds by allowing the princes to lower Jeremiah down into a cistern (Jeremiah 38:1-6).

Zedekiah once again changes his attitude towards Jeremiah when the Egyptian eunuch, Ebedmelech, asks permission to save Jeremiah from the cistern, which Zedekiah permits. Once raised out of the pit, Jeremiah returns to live in the court of the guard. There, Zedekiah questions Jeremiah with the hope of knowing what will happen in the future. Jeremiah prophecies that if Zedekiah submits to the Babylonians, then Zedekiah and his family will live.

---

[18] Newman and Stine, 1; Dorsey, 244.

If he does not, then Zedekiah will suffer greatly at the hands of the Babylonians, his family will be humiliated, and the holy city of Jerusalem will be set on fire. The following chapter, thirty-nine, describes the burning of Jerusalem, the gouging out of the eyes of Zedekiah, and the deportation of the people Jerusalem, with the exception of very poor people.

Chapters forty through forty-five shift the attention from the deported to the people who were left behind in Jerusalem along with Jeremiah, who supports the Babylonian appointed ruler, Gedaliah. Ishmael rises up against Gedaliah overthrows him, kills him along with many of his supporters and Babylonian guards. In fear of Babylonian retaliation, the military commanders ask Jeremiah to discern what to do. Once again Jeremiah tells them to remain in Jerusalem, submit to Babylonian rule, not to fear the Babylonian king and trust in God (Jeremiah 42). Ignoring Jeremiah, leaders of the Jewish people insist on fleeing to Egypt, which they do while forcing Jeremiah and Baruch to accompany them (Jeremiah 43).

As explained by Benedict XVI, Romans and the First Letter of Peter build upon Jeremiah insistence that the Jewish people recognize "the divine origin of the legal ordering of the state … [without] divinizing the state itself."[19] Romans commands: "Let every person be subject to the governing authorities. For there is no authority except from God, and those that exist have been instituted by God. Therefore, he who resists the authorities resists what God has appointed, and those who resist will incur judgment (Romans 13:1-2 *RSVCE*)." Similarly, Peter writes, "Be subject for the Lord's sake to every human institution, whether it be to the emperor as supreme, or to governors as sent by him to punish those who do wrong and to praise those who do right (1 Peter 2:13-14 *RSVCE*)."

---

[19] Joseph Ratzinger, *Values in a Time of Upheaval: Meeting the Challenges of the Future*, trans. Brian McNeil (San Francisco: Ignatius Press, 2006), Kindle location, 169 of 2245.

Section Questions

1. After Gedaliah is killed and the Jewish people flee Jerusalem for Egypt where do Jeremiah and Baruch go and why?

Punishment of the Nations (46:1-51:64) and Jerusalem Falls (52:1-34)[20]

These chapters entail prophecies of judgment and punishment of non-Jewish nations, ending with the Babylonian empire. Within these prophecies are also divine promises that at least some of the nations will be restored after they undergo punishment, specifically Moab (Jeremiah 48:47), the Ammonites (Jeremiah 49:6), and the Elam (Jeremiah 49:39).

The book concludes with chapter fifty-two, which summarizes King Zedekiah's humiliation at the hands of the Babylonians, the sack and burning of Jerusalem, and the deportation of Jewish people to Babylon.

Despite the sad tone of Jeremiah in describing these tragic notes, Jeremiah ends his prophetic book, Bergsma and Pitre observe, on a positive note. The last four verses describe the Judean King Jehoiachin's release from prison by the Babylonian king Evilmerodach, who mercifully permitted Jehoiachin to eat "at the king's table". In addition, Jehoiachin was given "a regular allowance ... until the day of his death as long as he lives (Jeremiah 52:33-34 *RSVCE*)." This kind treatment was part of God's subtle, providential ways of guiding history in fulfillment of His promise, Bergsma and Pitre add, of "good figs (Jeremiah 24:5 *RSVCE*)" among the people in exile in the land of the Babylonians:[21]

I will set my eyes upon them for good, and I will bring them back to

---

[20] Newman and Stine, 1; Dorsey, 244.

[21] Bergsma and Pitre, Kindle Location, 17164.

this land. I will build them up, and not tear them down; I will plant them, and not uproot them. I will give them a heart to know that I am the LORD; and they shall be my people and I will be their God, for they shall return to me with their whole heart (Jeremiah 24:6-7 *RSVCE*).

Section Questions

1. How specifically does Jeremiah end on a note of hope? Include in your answer the following: Moab, Ammonites, Elam, Jehoiachin.

Lamentations

Lamentations has traditionally been attributed to Jeremiah. Sometimes, the following verse from Chronicles is cited as supporting this attribution, "Jeremiah also uttered a lament for Josiah; and all the singing men and singing women have spoken of Josiah in their laments to this day. They made these an ordinance in Israel; behold, they are written in the Laments (2 Chronicles 35:25 *RSVCE*)." However, as David Clines comments, this verse does not well support the attribution to Jeremiah since Lamentations never refers to King Josiah.[1] Whether or not Jeremiah authored the book does not affect the inspired character of the book, since the primary author is God.

The time that Lamentations describes is the fall and burning of Jerusalem, including the temple, by the Babylonians in c. 587 B.C. The horror of this event is captured in five poetic laments: chapter one, chapter two, chapter three, chapter four, and chapter five.

The first lament, chapter one, mourns the destruction of Jerusalem. The city is depicted as a woman, "daughter of Zion (Lamentations 1:6 *RSVCE*)" who is "like a widow (Lamentations 1:1 *RSVCE*)" and is unfaithful in love: "I called to my lovers but they deceived me (Lamentations 1:9 *RSVCE*)."

The second lament, chapter two, describes God punishing the rebellious inhabitants of Jerusalem as warned. Daughter Zion is told to "Cry aloud to the Lord!... Should women eat their offspring ... Should priest and prophet be slain in the sanctuary of the Lord? (Lamentations 2:18, 20 *RSVCE*)."

---

[1] A.R. Pete Diamond, David J.A. Clines, *Commentary on the Bible: Jeremiah and Lamentations* (Grand Rapids: William B. Eerdmans Publishing Company, 2003).

This second lament is followed by chapter three, the third lament, which affirms that the love of the Lord is everlasting for God is merciful: "The steadfast love of the Lord never ceases, his mercies never come to an end.... The Lord is my portion, says my soul, 'therefore I will hope in him Lamentations 3:22, 24 *RSVCE*).'" Despite the intense suffering the Jewish people are experiencing as their city is destroyed and the people tortured and killed without mercy by the Babylonians, they are encouraged to maintain their faith in the goodness of God who "is good to those who wait for him, to the soul that seeks him. It is good that one should wait quietly for the salvation of the LORD (Lamentations 3:25-26 *RSVCE*)."

Trusting in God's goodness despite the trials one is experiencing, comments McConville, is a consistent theme in the Old Testament. A prime

---

[2] Rembrandt / Public domain, "Jeremiah Lamenting the Destruction of Jerusalem (Rembrandt)," https://commons.wikimedia.org/wiki/File: Rembrandt_Harmensz._van_Rijn_-_Jeremia_treurend_over_de_ verwoesting_van_Jeruzalem_-_Google_Art_Project.jpg.

example is Abraham who trusted that God would give him a child, and a child was born of Sarah when Abraham was one hundred years old. Abraham continued to trust God even when God commanded Abraham to offer his son "as a burnt offering (Genesis 22:2 *RSVCE*)." At the last moment, God tells Abraham to substitute a ram instead. Job is another example of one who retains his faith in God's goodness despite being afflicted in many severe ways. Yet another example, McConville cites along with Job, is Psalm 23 on the Good Shepherd, representing God, "Even though I walk through the valley of the shadow of death, I fear no evil; for you are with me; your rod and your staff, they comfort me (Psalm 23:4 *RSVCE*)."[3]

---

[3] Gordon J. McConville, *Exploring the Old Testament: A Guide to the Prophets: 4 Exploring the Bible Series* (Downers Grove: InterVarsity Press, 2002), 79-80.

[4] Julius Schnorr von Carolsfeld / Public domain, "The lamentations of Jeremiah are depicted in this 1860 woodcut by Julius Schnorr von Karolsfeld,"

Lamentations assures us that those who in faithful love patiently suffer from the trials and tribulations of this life will experience God's healing mercy: "For the Lord will not cast off forever, but, though he cause grief, he will have compassion according to the abundance of his steadfast love (Lamentations 3:31-32 *RSVCE*)." In commenting on these verses Ambrose writes, "Is it not evident that the Lord Jesus is angry with us when we sin in order that he may convert us through fear of his indignation? His indignation, then, is not the carrying out of vengeance but rather the working out of forgiveness."[5] Ambrose also explains that God calls us to repentance and lamentations so "that he may spare us those that shall be eternal."[6] Relatively brief, passing moments of sorrow on earth are nothing compared to the happiness of heaven or the sorrow of being separated from God for all eternity by being fixated on self-love to the exclusive of love of others, above all God.

Chapter four's lament focuses on divine punishment that God allows us to experience so that we will be given multiple opportunities to turn freely towards his healing, saving grace. This lament contains a reference to "the Lord's anointed (Lamentations 4:20 *RSVCE*)," a Messiah (*Mashiah*, מָשִׁיחַ) who "was taken in their pits, he of whom we said, 'Under his shadow we shall live among the nations (Lamentation 4:20 *RSVCE*).'" Church Fathers and early Christian writers interpreted this verse as fulfilled in Jesus whose, writes Origin, "flesh is called his shadow."[7] The human author of Lamentation may, states Bergsma and Pitre, intended this verse to refer to the anointed King

---

https://commons.wikimedia.org/wiki/File:Schnorr_von_Carolsfeld_Bibel_i n_Bildern_1860_141.png.

[5] Dean O. Wenthe, *Ancient Christian Commentary on Scripture: Old Testament XII Jeremiah, Lamentations* (Downers Grove, InterVarsity Press, 2009), 302. Ambrose's *Concerning Repentance* 1.5.22-24 is cited.

[6] Wenthe, 303. Ambrose's *Concerning Repentance* 1.5.22-24 is cited.

[7] Wenthe, 314. Origin's *Homilies on Joshua* 8.4 is cited.

Zedekiah who was exiled to Babylon. If this is the case, then Zedekiah as an imperfect anointed king points to the perfect anointed king, Jesus.[8]

Lamentations concludes with chapter five that beseeches God for mercy, "Remember, O Lord, what has befallen us; behold, and see our disgrace! … Restore us to yourself, O LORD, that we may be restored! Renew our days as of old! Or have you utterly rejected us? Are you exceedingly angry with us? (Lamentations 5:1,21-22 *RSVCE*)." The last verse of Lamentation, verse twenty-two, is a rhetorical question, since earlier Lamentations professes faith that God "will not cast off forever, but, though he cause grief, he will have compassion according to the abundance of his steadfast love (Lamentations 3:31-32 *RSVCE*)."

Section Questions

1. Traditionally, who is Lamentations attributed to?
2. What is the event and time that Lamentations mourns?
3. How does Lamentations both present mourning and trust in Providence?

---

[8] John Bergsma and Brant Pitre, *A Catholic Introduction to the Bible, Volume I* (San Francisco: Ignatius Press, 2018), Kindle Location, 17683.

Baruch

Traditionally, the book Baruch is attributed to Baruch, the secretary of Jeremiah. Modern scholars typically maintain that Baruch was not written by Baruch but rather consists of a variety of writings that were put together,

---

[1] Gustave Doré / Public domain, "An image of Baruch from Gustave Doré's illustrations for La Grande Bible de Tours," https://commons.wikimedia.org/wiki/File:Baruch.jpg.

possibly by Baruch.[2] As identified by Hahn, Baruch is comprised of five parts: Introduction (1:1-14), Confession of Sins and Prayer for Deliverance (1:15-3:8), Mosaic Law and Wisdom (3:9-4:4), Lamentation (4:4-5:9), Jeremiah's Letter against Idolatry (6).[3]

In the introduction, Baruch states that he composed the book when the Babylonians conquered Jerusalem, burned it, and deported its people. This is followed by a confession that "we have sinned before the Lord and have disobeyed him (Baruch 1:17-18 *RSVCE*)." Baruch pleads for God "to hear now the prayer of the dead of Israel of the sons of those who sinned before you, who did not heed the voice of Lord their God (Baruch 3:4 *RSVCE*)." The intense suffering the people of Judah are experiencing coupled with the intercessory prayer of the dead, asserts Baruch, are God's way of calling them to obey "his voice, to walk in the statutes of the Lord (Baruch 3:10 *RSVCE*)."

Baruch prophecies through the voice of Moses that while the Jewish people are in exile "they will come to themselves" for God will "give them a heart that obeys and ears that hear (Baruch 2:30-31 *RSVCE*)." God also one day will "make an everlasting covenant with them to be their God and they shall be my people; and I will never again remove my people Israel from the land which I have given them (Baruch 2:35 *RSVCE*)."

Chapter three then refers to a wisdom that will appear "upon earth…. She is the book of the commandments of God, and the law that endures forever (Baruch 3:37-4:1 *RSVCE*)." Church Fathers interpreted these verses as fulfilled in Jesus who as the fullness of wisdom was born in time and dwelt among human beings. As Irenaeus writes, "The prophets, receiving the prophetic gift from the same Word, announced his advent according to the

---

[2] Scott Hahn, *Catholic Bible Dictionary* (New York: Doubleday, 2009), 97.

[3] Hahn, 97.

flesh, by which the blending and communion of God and man took place."[4]

Chapter four and five integrate deep sorrow for the evil the people have committed with the certain hope that God will never totally abandon them, "For he who brought these calamities upon you will deliver you from the hand of your enemies (Baruch 4:18 *RSVCE*)." Baruch concludes with a letter by Jeremiah that condemns idolatry, including sex with temple prostitutes who falsely promise mystical union with a god by means of the sexual relations (Baruch 6:43-44).

Section Questions

1. What is the event and time that Baruch is on and who is Baruch?
2. In chapter 6, Baruch condemns temple prostitution. How is this related to idolatry?

---

[4] Sever J. Voicu, *Ancient Christian Commentary on Scripture: Old Testament XV, Apocrypha* (Downers Grove: IVP Academic: 2010), 478. Irenaeus's *On the Trinity* 4.42 is cited.

Ezekiel

Introduction

Unlike other books of the Bible, Bergsma and Pitre write:

> both ancient and contemporary commentators are largely agreed
> upon the fact that the book of Ezekiel is what it presents itself to be:
> the work of the prophet and priest Ezekiel, whose public ministry
> took place at the time of the Babylonian exile. Indeed, in the case of
> Ezekiel, the ordinary situation is reversed: while ancient rabbinic
> tradition held that "the men of the Great Synagogue wrote Ezekiel",
> many modern scholars think the book was (for the most part)
> actually composed by the prophet himself![1]

Ezekiel's Hebrew name is *Yechezqel* (יְחֶזְקֵאל). The name is made up by
two words *el* (אֵל) meaning God and *chazaq* (חָזַק) a root word signifying
strength.[2] In accordance with the meaning of his name, Ezekiel preaches a
message to strengthen the people of Judah during their time of exile in
Babylon.

Andreas Hoeck and Laurie W. Manhardt divide Ezekiel's prophecies to
his exiled people in six ways: Ezekiel's Call (chapters 1-3), Jerusalem Warned

---

[1] John Bergsma and Brant Pitre, *A Catholic Introduction to the Bible,
Volume I* (San Francisco: Ignatius Press, 2018), Kindle Location 18417.

[2] "3168, Strong's Concordance, Yechezqel," biblehub.com,
https://biblehub.com/hebrew/3168.htm.

(chapters 4-11), Israel's Exile (chapter 12-19), Israel's Unfaithfulness (chapters 20-24), Judgements Against Nations (chapters 25-32), Israel Restored (chapters 33-39), and A Renewed Israel (chapters 40-48).[3]

Section Questions

1. Contrast a Rabbinic Tradition on who authored Ezekiel with the dominant modern view.

2. What is does the name Ezekiel *Yechezqel* (יְחֶזְקֵאל) mean in Hebrew?

---

[3] Andreas Hoeck, and Laurie Watson Manhardt, *Ezekiel, Hebrews, Revelation* (Steubenville: Emmaus Road Publishing, 2010), ii.

[4] Copy by unknown artist after illustration by Matthaeus (Matthäus) Merian the elder (1593-1650) / Public domain, "One traditional depiction of the cherubim and chariot vision, based on the description by Ezekiel," https://commons.wikimedia.org/wiki/File:Ezekiel%27s_vision.jpg.

Ezekiel's Call Chapters 1-3

In the first chapter, Ezekiel identifies himself as "Ezekiel the priest" who accompanies the Babylonian exiles by a river where he sees divine visions. These visions inform his complementary role as prophet. In the first vision, he sees four brightly gleaming creatures united together in a fire. Although each had similar looking wings and human looking bodies, they had different faces: human, lion, ox, and eagle. These four creatures have been interpreted as representing the four evangelists: Matthew, Mark, Luke, and John. Both Jerome and Gregory the Great identify the human faced creature with Matthew, the lion faced creature with Mark, the ox faced creature with Luke and the eagle faced creature with John. Gregory the Great writes:

> The preface of each Gospel avers that these four-winged creatures denote the four holy Evangelists. Because he began from the generations of humankind, Matthew is justly represented by a man; because of the crying in the wilderness, Mark is rightly indicated by a lion; because he started from a sacrifice, Luke is well described as an ox; and because he begins with the divinity of the Word, John is worthily signified by an eagle, he who says, "In the beginning was the Word, and the Word was with God, and the Word was God"; while he stretched towards the very substance of divinity, he fixed his eye on the sun as if in the fashion of an eagle. But because all the elect are members of our Savior, for our Savior is indeed the head of all the elect, in that his members are thereby depicted, there is no obstacle to even him being signified in all these. For the only-begotten Son of God truly became man; he deigned to die like an ox at sacrifice for our salvation; he, through the virtue of his fortitude, rose as a lion. Moreover, the lion is said to sleep with open eyes because, in the very death in which our Savior could sleep through his humanity, by remaining immortal in his divinity, he kept vigil.

Furthermore, ascending to heaven after his resurrection, he was carried aloft to the heights like an eagle. He is therefore wholly the same within us at the same time, who became a man by being born, an ox in dying, a lion in rising again and an eagle in ascending to the heavens.[5]

After encountering these strange creatures, the LORD speaks to him and commissions Ezekiel to preach to the "sons of Israel, to a nation of rebels.... And you shall speak my words to them, whether they hear or refuse to hear (Ezekiel 2:3,7 *RSVCE*)." As God speaks to him, Ezekiel sees a hand reaching out to him. The hand is holding a scroll with writing on it. Ezekiel is commanded, in a similar as John will be commanded in the book of Revelation (Revelation 10:9-10) "eat what is offered to you; eat this scroll, and go, speak to the house of Israel (Ezekiel 3:1 *RSVCE*)."

Section Questions

1. According to Jerome and Gregory the Great which faces of the four faced creature corresponds to which Evangelist and why?

Jerusalem Warned Chapters 4-11

This section opens with God ordering Ezekiel to "portray" on a brick a miniature model of Jerusalem. God then tells Ezekiel to destroy the model with a plate of iron, representing the coming Babylonian siege (Ezekiel 4:1-3 *RSVCE*). God also commands Ezekiel to do a number of other symbolic acts

---

[5] Kenneth Stevenson and Michael Glerup, *Ancient Christian Commentary on Scripture: Old Testament XIII, Ezekiel, Daniel* (Downers Grove: IVP Academic: 2008), 27. Gregory the Great's *Homilies on Ezekiel* 1.4.1. is cited.

which prophetically warn the people Jerusalem to stop doing evil and instead repent. If they fail to repent, God will punish them by allowing history to take its corrective course. In obedience, Ezekiel sleeps on his side for 430 days (390 on his left and 40 on his right) and bakes a barley cake on human excrement. After Ezekiel protests doing the latter symbolic act, God allows him to bake the cake over cow dung (Ezekiel 4:4-17 *RSVCE*).

In the following chapter, Ezekiel again symbolically does acts that represent how the people of Jerusalem will suffer. He shaves his head, weighs the shaved hair, burns a third of his hair in a "fire in the midst of the city (Ezekiel 5:2 *RSVCE*)," strikes another third of his hair with a sword, and throws the remainder into the wind. In the subsequent chapter, Ezekiel preaches against Israel's idolatrous practices that will bring down God's anger upon them. Speaking for God, Ezekiel says, "Thus I will spend my fury upon them. And you shall know that I am the LORD, when their slain lie among their idols round about their altars (Ezekiel 6:13 *RSVCE*)." The reason for God's anger is due to Israel's lust for silver and gold that "cannot satisfy their hunger (Ezekiel 7:19 *RSVCE*)," "vainglory (Ezekiel 7:20 *RSVCE*)," idolatry, and "bloody crimes (Ezekiel 7:23 *RSVCE*)."

The next three chapters (8-11) describe a vision that Ezekiel sees. In the vision a brightly gleaming divine being "that had the appearance of a man (Ezekiel 8:2 *RSVCE*)," shows Ezekiel the inside of the holy Jerusalem Temple. Ezekiel is shocked to see the people of Judah engaged in worship of idols right inside the Temple, including by "seventy men of the elders of the house of Israel (Ezekiel 8:11 *RSVCE*)." In response, God sends six men armed with swords to kill all in Jerusalem except for those who "sigh and groan over all the abominations (Ezekiel 9:4 *RSVCE*)" committed in the city. After the executioners complete their mission, angels appear including cherubim each with four faces: human, lion, ox, and eagle. (Ezekiel 10)

Finally, in chapter eleven God gives Ezekiel the task to both warn of impending punishment and to console with a message of redemption that will come after the punishment. In the latter message of hope, God, through

Ezekiel, promises that one day He will restore Israel by gathering them from the nations they are scattered in. Upon gathering them, God promises, "I will give them one heart, and put a new spirit within them; I will take the stony heart out of their flesh and give them a heart of flesh, that they may walk in my statues and keep my ordinances and obey them; and they shall be my people, and I will be their God (Ezekiel 11:19-20 *RSVCE*)." Followers of Christ believe that the new heart and new spirit is the heart of Jesus Christ which as the center of His Mystical Body is given to all the baptized to participate in, to share in.

McConville cautions against interpreting Ezekiel's reference to "a religion of the heart" in an overly modern individualistic manner since the heart of flesh in the text represents God's chosen people taken together as they abide by God's commandments similar to Deuteronomy's commandment to Israel as a whole to, "Hear, O Israel…. you shall love the Lord your God with all your heart (Deuteronomy 6:4-5 *RSVCE*)."[6] Similarly, St Paul writes, "Now you (plural you, *humeis*, ὑμεῖς) are the body of Christ and individually members of it 1 Corinthians 12:27 *RSVCE*)."

As a body of Christ, our identity is defined socially, in relationship with others who also make up the body of Christ. This means, as Benedict XVI explains, the condition for true freedom is living in accordance with our social, relational nature. Living in accordance with our social nature necessarily entails, writes Benedict XVI, a "shared freedom, freedom in a coexistence of other freedoms, which are mutually limiting and thus mutually supportive."[7]

---

[6] Gordon J. McConville, *Exploring the Old Testament: A Guide to the Prophets: 4 Exploring the Bible Series* (Downers Grove: InterVarsity Press, 2002), 103.

[7] Joseph Cardinal Ratzinger, *Truth and Tolerance: Christian Belief and World Religions*, trans. H. Taylor (San Francisco: Ignatius Press, 2004), 247-249.

In his dual role as prophet and priest, Ezekiel criticizes priests who practice formal, communal expressions of worship without limiting their desires for the goods of this world by taking into account the needs of others. The Ten Commandments are the essential standard which helps one to discern when to limit a desire. As interpreted in relationship with our social nature, since the Ten Commandments, writes Benedict XVI, "are the answer to the inner demands of our nature, then they are not at the opposite pole to our freedom but are rather the concrete form it takes. They are then the foundation for every law of freedom and are the one truly liberating power in human history."[8] The Ten Commandments by themselves, though, do not give the ability to live in accordance with their socially moral teaching. Jesus gives us this ability by offering to us a participation in His perfect heart and mind by Baptism.

In interpreting Ezekiel's prophecy of a new heart and new mind Benedict XVI points to Jesus:

> To renew man, the Lord — alluding to these prophetic voices which always guided Israel towards the clarity of monogamy — recognized with Ezekiel that, to live this vocation, we need a new heart; instead of a heart of stone — as Ezekiel said — we need a heart of flesh, a heart that is truly human.
>
> And the Lord "implants" this new heart in us at baptism, through faith. It is not a physical transplant, but perhaps we can make this comparison. After a transplant, the organism needs treatment, requires the necessary medicines to be able to live with the new heart, so that it becomes "one's own heart" and not the "heart of another."

---

[8] Benedict XVI, *Day by Day with Pope Benedict XVI*, ed. Peter John Cameron (San Francisco: Ignatius Press, 2006), 37.

This is especially so in this "spiritual transplant" when the Lord implants within us a new heart, a heart open to the Creator, to God's call. To be able to live with this new heart, adequate treatment is necessary; one must have recourse to the appropriate medicines so that it can really become "our heart."

Thus, by living in communion with Christ, with his Church, the new heart truly becomes "our own heart" and makes marriage possible. The exclusive love between a man and a woman, their life as a couple planned by the Creator, becomes possible, even if the atmosphere of our world makes it difficult to the point that it appears impossible.

The Lord gives us a new heart and we must live with this new heart, using the appropriate therapies to ensure that it is really "our own." In this way we live with all that the Creator has given us and this creates a truly happy life.[9]

The "medicines" that we need to avail ourselves in order to accept the new heart of Jesus Christ are above all given through the Sacraments, especially the Eucharist and Sacrament of Reconciliation, by which Jesus extends his saving, healing, merciful presence in time.

Section Questions

1. How is the new heart promised in chapter eleven fulfilled by Jesus and by us? Include the following in your response: Mystical Body, Heart of Jesus, Our Hearts, Heart Transplant, Sacraments.

---

[9] Benedict XVI, "We Must Make God Present Again in Our Society, April 23, 2006," zenit.org, https://zenit.org/articles/pope-s-q-amp-a-with-young-people-part-1/.

Israel's Exile Chapters 12-19

In chapter twelve, God commands Ezekiel to act as one going into exile. This symbolic acting would likely have involved, comments Bergsma and Pitre, Ezekiel leaving his home naked, since those forced into exile would typically be humiliated by being forced to strip naked. Interestingly, the Hebrew root word for exile (גָּלָה *galah*) also means removed, uncovered, stripped bare since it was common for those who were forcibly deported to be stripped naked.[10]

After dramatically acting out the exile of the people of Jerusalem, Ezekiel then issues a series of condemnations. He condemns lying, false prophets, "they misled my people, saying, 'Peace,' when there is no peace (Ezekiel 13:10 *RSVCE*)." The condemnation of false prophets is followed by the condemnation of idolatry. Here, Ezekiel acting in his role as the conscience of his people, as Robert D. Miller phrases it, exhorts a return to worship of the one true God. Archaeological finds in Jerusalem, Miller states, indicate that idolatry had become common even in the holy Temple of Jerusalem. He writes:

> [O]ur traditional, ideal view of the Temple doesn't square with some passages in the Bible. For instance, in 2 Kings, when King Josiah reforms the Temple, he has to remove all sorts of strange religious paraphernalia and installations that were never in Solomon's design. We know these "aberrations" from archaeology as well. There are figurines that archaeologists call "Pillar Women"—about 5 inches tall with gigantic breasts that they hold up with their hands—and these are unique to Judah. Meaning they're not borrowed from some

---

[10] "1540. galah," biblehub.com, https://biblehub.com/hebrew/1540.htm. John Bergsma and Brant Pitre, *A Catholic Introduction to the Bible, Volume I* (San Francisco: Ignatius Press, 2018), Kindle Location 18168.

foreign religion. Although found all over Judah, half of them were recovered in Jerusalem, many only a short distance from the Temple.[11]

According to the chronology of the first chapter, Ezekiel was born around the time King Josiah (c. 640-609 B.C.) began reforming the Temple, which was about thirty years before King Jehoiachin was deported along with the people of Jerusalem in 597 B.C. This means that Ezekiel would likely have seen many false idols in the Temple, including the big breasted Pillar Women that have been uncovered by archaeologists.

In chapters fifteen and sixteen, God, through Ezekiel, compares the people of Jerusalem to an unfruitful vine whose only use is to be "given to the fire for fuel (Ezekiel 15:4 *RSVCE*)," and to a promiscuous woman who "slaughtered my children and delivered them up as an offering by fire to them (Ezekiel 16:21 *RSVCE*)." Child sacrifice to the false God Molech was practiced both in Israel and in Judah and for this reason was explicitly banned:[12] "You shall not give any of your children to devote them by fire to Molech (Leviticus 18:21 *RSVCE*)." King Josiah, under whose rule Ezekiel lived, attempted to end this horrific practice by destroying "Topheth, which is in the valley of the sons of Hinnom, that no one might burn his son or his daughter as an offering to Molech (2 Kings 23:10 *RSVCE*)."

Even a Judean King, King Manasseh, who preceded Josiah, "burned his sons as an offering in the valley of the son of Hinnom (2 Chronicles 33:6 *RSVCE*)." Clearly, argue Bergsma and Pitre, Ezekiel is applying an image of promiscuous woman who is punished for her sins by her own lovers metaphorically to the people of Judah and Israel and is not laying "out

---

[11] Robert D. Miller II, *Understanding the Old Testament* (Chantilly: The Teaching Company, 2019), 211.

[12] Scott Hahn, *Catholic Bible Dictionary* (New York: Doubleday, 2009), 624.

guideless for male-female interaction in society."[13] Furthermore, add Bergsma and Pitre, in the last verses of chapter sixteen God even though the Judean people have been faithless like a promiscuous woman who repeatedly engages in adulterous relations, "yet I will remember by covenant with you in the days of your youth, and will establish with you an everlasting covenant ... [and] forgive you all that you have done (Ezekiel 16:60, 63 *RSVCE*)."[14] An example that foreshadows this time of divine merciful faithfulness is when the evil King Manasseh repented of his ways while in captivity in Babylon "and God received his entreaty and heard his supplication and brought him again to Jerusalem into his kingdom. Then Manasseh knew that the Lord was God (2 Chronicles 33:13 *RSVCE*)."

Chapter seventeen contains yet another metaphor in which Israel is compared to a cedar tree whose top is fought over by two giant eagles, one representing Babylon and the other Egypt. Each wants to claim tree's top for itself. One day, though, God promises, "I myself will take a sprig from the lofty top of the cedar ... and ... plant it upon a high and loft mountain ... and under it will dwell all kinds of beasts; in the shade of its branches birds of every sort will nest (Ezekiel 17:22-23 *RSVCE*)." For Catholics, this mighty tree which provides security for all is the Catholic Church which by being wedded to Jesus Christ provides for all the security of true faith and true love in, under, and among its many branches.

Two more chapters follow after seventeen which conclude this section. In chapter eighteen Ezekiel exhorts to repentance both the "wicked man" and the "righteous man" who always potentially can fall from his upright ways. He concludes the section in chapter nineteen by lamenting for his beloved Israel.

---

[13] Bergsma and Pitre, Kindle Location 18214.

[14] Bergsma and Pitre, Kindle Location 18214.

Section Questions

1. How can Ezekiel's vision of two eagles fighting over the top of a cedar tree be spiritually interpreted as fulfilled in the Catholic Church? Include the following in your response: Transplanted, Shade

Israel's Unfaithfulness Chapters 20-24

Chapters twenty through twenty-four focus on the sins of Israel. Israel is once again compared with an unfaithful woman who, "became more and more promiscuous as she recalled the days of her youth, when she was a prostitute in Egypt. There she lusted after her lovers, whose genitals were like those of donkeys and whose emission was like that of horses (Ezekiel 23:19-20 *NIV*)." The infidelity that Ezekiel describes begins in chapter twenty with the Exodus of the Israelites out of Egypt to the Promised Land. It includes the various ways that Israel was an unfaithful spouse in the following times: during the Exodus journey (chapter 20), after settling in the Promised Land (chapter 22), and during the Assyrian and Babylonian deportations (chapter 23). The section concludes with Ezekiel's wife dying in chapter twenty-four as yet another sign of impending punishment. God commands Ezekiel not to mourn for his wife's death for her death symbolizes Jerusalem, God's spiritual bride, dying by being overtaken by pagan conquerors. After Jerusalem's spiritual death, her people also will not mourn for her as they, comment Bergsma and Pitre, "will be struggling merely to survive."[15]

In the midst of this marital interpretation of salvation history, Ezekiel refers to laws that God gave that are not good: "Moreover I gave them statutes that were not good and ordinances by which they could not have life (Ezekiel 20:25 *RSVCE*)." In their explanation of this verse, Bergsma and Pitre cite Jesus who in describing the bad law of divorce that God permitted said,

---

[15] Bergsma and Pitre, Kindle Location 18289.

"For your hardness of heart Moses allowed you to divorce your wives, but from the beginning it was not so (Matthew 19:8 *RSVCE*)." Other bad laws that Deuteronomy (meaning second law in Greek) permitted in contrast with the preceding books of Leviticus and Numbers are, identifies Bergsma and Pitre, "*herem* war against the Canaanites (Deuteronomy 20:16-18), [and] captive wives (Deut 21:10-14)."[16] God also tolerated a relaxation of laws concerning worship including allowing other animals besides the firstborn to be sacrificed (Leviticus 27:10, 26, 33; Deuteronomy 14:23-26).[17]

Another way to interpret the verse is in reference to St. Paul who writes in his letter to the Galatians, "For all who rely on works of the law are under a curse.... Now it is evident that no man is justified before God by the law (3:10-11 *RSVCE*)." Here, St. Paul is pointing to Jesus who is the fulfillment of law in person and who invites all to participate in His perfect life which enables one to also fulfill the law, something that no one is capable of doing by simply following the law in an external manner. All laws before the coming of Jesus Christ, therefore, are in a certain sense not good since they only state what to do and what not to do without giving the ability to practice the law. This ability only can come from a relationship with God, from a participation in God (2 Peter 1:4) who alone is good (Mark 10:18)

Section Questions

1. Why does God command Ezekiel not to mourn the death of Ezekiel's wife?
2. How are the following examples of Ezekiel's laws that are not good (Ezekiel 20:25)? Herem War, Some Laws in Deuteronomy.
3. With respect to divorce, how does Jesus end the laws that are not

---

[16] Bergsma and Pitre, Kindle Location 18550.

[17] Bergsma and Pitre, Kindle Location 18550. Bergsma and Pitre compare Leviticus 27:10, 26, 33 with Deuteronomy 14:23-26.

good mentioned by Ezekiel?

Judgments Against Nations Chapters 25-32

Chapter twenty-five through chapter   thirty-two   contains   multiple prophecies of judgments against Gentile nations and people: Ammonites, Moab, Edom, Philistines, Tyre, Sidon, and Egypt. The prophecy concerning Tyre is particularly interesting since it states that the King of Tyre was in the Garden of Eden, was dazzling beautiful, was once "the signet of perfection (Ezekiel 28:13 *RSVCE*)," was morally "blameless (Ezekiel 28:15 *RSVCE*)," and was a companion of the angels. Despite all these good qualities the King of Tyre became "filled with violence and... sinned (Ezekiel 28:16 *RSVCE*). The sin that brought about this downfall was the spiritual sin of pride and not a sin of the flesh. "Your heart was proud because of your beauty; you corrupted your wisdom for the sake of your splendor. I cast you to the ground (Ezekiel 28:17 *RSVCE*)."

Since the King of Tyre is not an angel, did not live in the Garden of Eden before the Fall of Adam and Eve why does the passage compare the king to a fallen angel? One possible answer is that the passage is not identifying the king with a fallen angel but is only comparing the king to a fallen angel as a way to emphasize how evil the king had become. Another answer, provided by Bergsma and Pitre, is although the passage is not identifying the king with a fallen angel it is not simply a comparison between the king and a fallen angel but rather is revealing the spiritual power behind the throne, the spiritual power that helps to explain why powerful rulers sometimes commit the most heinous, awful sins such as Pot Pot, Hitler and Stalin.[18] The explanation is that these powerful rulers became proud and through the door of their pride Satan entered into their hearts, took possession of them and they proceeded to use them as his tools of great evil in the world.

---

[18] Bergsma and Pitre, Kindle Location 18309.

Cyril of Jerusalem, in union with other Church Fathers, affirms that the later interpretation of the comparison:

> The chief author of sin, then, is the devil, the author of all evil. Not I but the Lord has said, "The devil sins from the beginning." Before him no one sinned. Nor did he sin because by nature he was of necessity prone to sin—or else the responsibility for sin would reflect on him who created him in this way—but after being created good, he became a devil by his own free choice, receiving that name from his action. Though he was an archangel, he was afterwards called devil (slanderer) from his slandering, and though he was once a good servant of God, he was afterwards rightly named Satan, for Satan is interpreted "the adversary." This is not my teaching but that of the inspired prophet Ezekiel. For taking up a lament against him, he says, "You were a seal of resemblance and crown of beauty; you were begotten in the paradise of God," and a little further on, "Blameless you were in your conduct from the day you were created until evil was found in you."[19]

Interpreting the verses canonically, that is recognizing God as the primary author of the Bible and consequently interpreting early books with later books, Ambrose asserts that the serpent described in Genesis who tempts Adam and Eve is the devil, "It follows that the serpent in paradise was certainly not brought into being without the will of God. In the figure of the serpent we see the devil. That the devil existed even in paradise we are informed by the prophet Ezekiel."[20] When Genesis is taken alone and not viewed in light of other books of Scripture then it is not evident that the

---

[19] Stevenson and Glerup, 209-210. Cyril of Jerusalem *Catechetical Lectures* 2.9 is cited.

[20] Stevenson and Glerup, 212. Ambrose's *On Paradise* 2.9 is cited.

serpent is the devil since Genesis 3, as Robert D. Miller argues "does not mention the devil or use the name Satan."[21] Nonetheless, since the Hebrew word used for serpent (*nahash*) is used, continues Miller, in other passages of the Bible, specifically Isaiah (27:1) and Amos (9:3) it means dragon which "Israel consistently uses…to symbolize evil. … That means that when Jewish and Christian tradition consider the serpent to be equivalent to the devil, the original authors already had some of that in mind."[22]

The desire of the devil to enter through the door of pride and use us as his instruments of disordered love, of his disordered love of power, glory, praise, and honor should be a warning to all and serve as a reminder that as Marcellino D'Ambrosio explains the sins of the flesh, such as sexual sins, are not the most dangerous sins. He writes:

> Fornication and adultery are serious sins indeed. In fact, they are expressions of one of the seven capital sins–lust. Many assume that lust is considered by Christianity to be the epitome of sin, the worst possible vice.
>
> Actually, in the hierarchy (or should I say "lowerarchy") of capital sins, the king-pin and most deadly of the seven sins is not lust but pride. Pride – the lust not for pleasure, but for honor, glory and power – is the "one ring that rules them all" in J. R. R. Tolkien's famous Trilogy.
>
> Lust wrongly seeks sexual pleasure apart from love and life. Pride seeks greatness apart from God. The tricky thing of pride is that it can often start in the course of promoting God's greatness.

---

[21] Miller, 55.

[22] Miller, 56.

Here's how it works–as people begin applauding as you do God's work, you think they are applauding for you. It's a rather pitiful mistake really. Imagine the donkey Jesus rode into Jerusalem thinking that the crowd had turned out for him!

Such applause, however, can be addicting. The proud person ultimately will do anything to make the ovation happen and keep it going. But there can only be one star. Pride is essentially competitive. So anyone who threatens to steal the show becomes a mortal enemy. Even if he happens to be God.

The proud man does not teach to enlighten, but rather to pontificate, to impress, to appear as the authority.[23]

Along the same lines Pope Francis asks, "What is the most dangerous attitude for every Christian life?" He then answers:

It is pride. It is the attitude of those who stand before God thinking that they always have their affairs in order with him: the proud think they have everything in order. …

There are sins that are seen and sins that are unseen. There are glaring sins that make noise but there are also sins that are devious, that lurk in our heart without us even noticing. The worst of these is pride, which can even infect people who live a profound religious life. There was once a well-known convent of nuns, in the 1600-

---

[23] Marcellino D'Ambrosio, "One Sin to Rule them All," crossroadsinitiave.com, https://www.crossroadsinitiative.com/media/articles/pride-of-the-pharisees/?inf_contact_key=186aab2aa618b8484077cb4c3fcc3a473f76f4106cff3f52679a05ce0f00d235.

1700s, at the time of Jansenism. They were utterly perfect, and it was said of them that they were really pure like angels, but also proud like demons. It is a bad thing. Sin divides fraternity; sin makes us imagine we are better than others; sin makes us think we are comparable to God.[24]

Sometimes, Aquinas teaches, God in his providential wisdom will permit a proud person to fall into a sexual sin so that the visible nature of the sexual sin will help to reveal to the person his much graver invisible spiritual sin of pride.[25]

---

[24] Francis, "General Audience, St. Peter's Square, Wednesday, 10 April 2019," vatican.va, http://www.vatican.va/content/francesco/en/audiences/ 2019/documents/papa-francesco_20190410_udienza-generale.html.

[25] Thomas Aquinas, "Summa Theologica," II-II, Q. 162, Art. 6, Ad. 3, newadvent.org, http://www.newadvent.org/summa/3162.htm. "Just as in syllogisms that lead to an impossible conclusion one is sometimes convinced by being faced with a more evident absurdity, so too, in order to overcome their pride, God punishes certain men by allowing them to fall into sins of the flesh, which though they be less grievous are more evidently shameful. Hence Isidore says (*De Summo Bono* ii, 38) that 'pride is the worst of all vices; whether because it is appropriate to those who are of highest and foremost rank, or because it originates from just and virtuous deeds, so that its guilt is less perceptible. on the other hand, carnal lust is apparent to all, because from the outset it is of a shameful nature: and yet, under God's dispensation, it is less grievous than pride. For he who is in the clutches of pride and feels it not, falls into the lusts of the flesh, that being thus humbled he may rise from his abasement.' From this indeed the gravity of pride is made manifest. For just as a wise physician, in order to cure a worse disease, allows the patient to contract one that is less dangerous, so the sin of pride is shown to be more

Section Questions

1. In chapter twenty-eight, verses 13-17, the King of Tyre is likened to
    a fallen angel. How does Cyril of Jerusalem interpret these verses?

Israel Restored Chapters 33-39

The prophecies of impending punishment is followed by the hopeful
message that after experiencing a fall and being scattered, Israel will one day

---

grievous by the very fact that, as a remedy, God allows men to fall into other
sins."

[26] Gustave Doré / Public domain, "The Vision of the Valley of the Dry
Bones,"   https://commons.wikimedia.org/wiki/File:The_Vision_of_The_
Valley_of_The_Dry_Bones.jpg.

be restored: "For thus says the Lord God: Behold, I, I myself will search for my sheep, and will seek them out. As a shepherd seeks out his flock when some of his sheep have been scattered abroad, so will I seek out my sheep; and I will rescue them from all places where they have been scattered (Ezekiel 34:11-12 *RSVCE*)."

Along with the above promise of a "New Exodus" (Ezekiel 34:11; 36:24), and a "New Creation" (Ezekiel 34:26-28; 36:11) as Pitre and Bergsma term it, God also promises a new "covenant of peace (Ezekiel 34:25 *RSVCE*) that is "everlasting" (Ezekiel 26 *RSVCE*), and the infusion of a "new heart" and "new spirit" (Ezekiel 26:26). The combination of both an uprooting from the past and continuity with the past is comments Pitre and Bergsma "*not* something that was only created during the New Covenant period."[27]

As Ezekiel prophecies, the promised new creation, peace, heart and spirit is not in total continuity with the past, in the sense of identity, but entails essential differences including what is dead (dry bones) comes to life (Ezekiel 37:1-14), and what was divided regains its original unity (37:15-23). In commenting on Ezekiel, John Chrysostom observes that when Ezekiel prophecies of God establishing "one shepherd, my servant David (Ezekiel 34:23)" over a united Israel, Ezekiel is speaking of a Davidic person and not about the patriarch David, "[f]or the patriarch David will not be raised up to shepherd the saints, but Christ."[28]

Ezekiel's divine promises are ultimately fulfilled in Jesus Christ, as the future Davidic King, as the new heart and new spirit who invites all to participate in His new heart and new spirit as members of His Mystical Body, as the new Moses and Joshua who lead people out from the slavery of sin into the promised land of the Kingdom of God that begins in this life by those who strive to live according to the New Law of the Holy Spirit governed by

---

[27] Bergsma and Pitre, Kindle Location 18579.

[28] Stevenson and Glerup, 242. John Chrysostom *Commentary on the Gospel of John* 1.146 is cited.

the Beatitudes as the fulfillment of the Ten Commandments, as the New Adam and New Creation who is born of the New Woman, Mary, the renewed and perfect "mother of all living (Genesis 3:20 *RSVCE*)," the New Eve.

Section Questions

1. How can the following prophecies be understood as fulfilled in Jesus: New Exodus (34:11-12); One Davidic Shepherd (34:23), New Creation (34:26-28; 36:11); Peace Covenant (34:25); Everlasting Covenant (26); New Heart/New Spirit (26:26)

A Renewed Israel Chapters 40-48

Ezekiel concludes with a vision of a new Temple in a renewed and perfected Israel. The first three chapters (40-43) describe the glorious details of the new Temple. Chapter forty-four continues with a vision in which Ezekiel is shown the "outer gate of the sanctuary, which faces east; and it was shut (Ezekiel 44:1 *RSVCE*)." Ezekiel is told, "This gate shall remain shut; it shall not be opened, and no one shall enter by it; for the LORD, the God of Israel, has entered by it; therefore, it shall remain shut (Ezekiel 44:2 *RSVCE*)."

Church Fathers interpreted these verses in reference to Mary who, according to ancient doctrine, remained a virgin before, during, and after giving birth to the Lord Jesus Christ. Representing Eastern Fathers, Theodoret of Cyr comments, "It is very likely that these words refer to the womb of the Virgin, through which no one enters and from which no one departs other than the only one who is the Lord."[29] Representing the Western Fathers, Ambrose asks, "What is that gate of the sanctuary, that outer gate

---

[29] Stevenson and Glerup, 242. Theodoret of Cyr *Commentary on Ezekiel* 16.44 is cited.

facing the east and remaining closed? Is not Mary the gate through whom the Redeemer entered this world?[30] Similarly, Jerome states, "Some people nobly understand the Virgin Mary as the door that is closed, who before and after birth remained a virgin, through which only the Lord God of Israel enters."[31]

At the Annunciation, Jesus the Lord God of Israel miraculously entered the Virgin Mary without disturbing her virginity, and Jesus was born from the Mary in a similar way as he rose from the dead without moving the stone away from the tomb (Matthew 28:2). As with the closed door of the Temple in Ezekiel vision, the door of Mary's womb is also closed since the only one who may enter her by miraculously passing through, without disturbance, her immaculate womb is God, Jesus Christ.

---

[30] Stevenson and Glerup, 242. Ambrose *Letter* 44 is cited.

[31] Stevenson and Glerup, 242. Jerome *Commentary on Ezekiel* 13.44.1-3 is cited.

[32] 18th century icon painter / Public domain, "Russian icon of the Prophet Ezekiel holding a scroll with his prophecy and pointing to the

Focusing on the Temple once again, chapter forty-seven describes life-giving water flowing from the temple. Understood in a Marian manner, the Temple foreshadows Mary as the new Eve, as the new "mother of all living (Genesis 3:20 *RSVCE*)." The water flowing out of her is Jesus, who, as Jesus promised the Samaritan woman, will give water of "eternal life (John 4:14 *RSVCE*)." John's gospel further states that as Jesus lay on the cross a soldier pierced Jesus' side with a spear and out flowed blood and water (John 19:34). This fulfilled Jesus' promise that his blood "is poured out for many for the forgiveness of sins (Matthew 26:28 *RSVCE*)." In addition, those deemed to be Jesus' sheep will be saved at "his right hand, but the goats at the left (Matthew 25:33 *RSVCE*)."

Interestingly, Ezekiel prophecies that the life-giving water flowing from the renewed Temple flows "down from below the right side of the threshold of the temple (Ezekiel 47:1 *RSVCE*)." According to Bergsma and Pitre, on the Feast of Tabernacles, one of the three feasts that required the Jewish men to make a pilgrimage to the Temple (Deuteronomy 16:16 *RSVCE*), "Jesus identifies *himself* as the source"[33] of this life-giving future water prophesied by Ezekiel: "On the last day of the feast, the great day, Jesus stood up and proclaimed, 'If any one thirst, let him come to me and drink. He who believes in me, as the Scripture has said, 'Out of his heart shall flow rivers of living water' (John 7:38 *RSVCE*)."

This interpretation is confirmed, assert Bergsma and Pitre, in "the book of Revelation" which:

> like Ezekiel before it, ends with a vision of an angel measuring the new Jerusalem and the new "Temple" (Rev 21-22). At the very climax of this vision, John describes a river of "the water of life"

"closed gate" (18th century, Iconostasis of Kizhi monastery, Russia)," https://commons.wikimedia.org/wiki/File:Ezekiel-icon.jpg.

[33] Bergsma and Pitre, Kindle Location 18616.

flowing from the "throne of God and the Lamb" in the heavenly city of Jerusalem, which is also the bride of Christ (Rev 21:1-2; 22:1).[34]

This "water of life" is the eternal life that flows forth from Christ to the Church, His Bride, as the extension of Christ's presence in time. We encounter these eternal waters especially through the Sacraments of the Church as Pope St. Leo the Great explains, "that which till then was visible of our Redeemer was changed into a sacramental presence, and that faith might be more excellent and stronger, sight gave way to doctrine, the authority of which was to be accepted by believing hearts enlightened with rays from above."[35]

Section Questions

1. According to Church Fathers, why is the outer closed eastern gate in Ezekiel's vision of chapter forty-four fulfilled in Mary?

2. How is Ezekiel's vision of life-giving water flowing out of the Temple fulfilled in Mary, the Church, and Jesus? Include the following in your response: Pierced Side, Feast of Tabernacles, Sacraments

---

[34] Bergsma and Pitre, Kindle Location 18625.

[35] Leo the Great, "Sermon 74, II," newadvent.org, http://www.newadvent.org/fathers/360374.htm.

Daniel

Introduction

The first verse situates the book of Daniel: "In the third year of the reign of Jehoiakim king of Judah, Nebuchadnezzar king of Babylon came to Jerusalem and besieged it (Daniel 1:1 *RSVCE*)." Since King Jehoiakim reigned from 609-598 B.C. this means that his third year is 606 B.C. McConville points out that this date is historically problematic by one year since in 605 B.C. the Babylonians defeated the Assyrians and Egyptian armies in 605 B.C. during the Battle of Carchemish and Nebuchadnezzar then became king of Babylon. An explanation could be, McConville offers, of "post-dating" events which means that "the third year of Jehoiakim would be 605."[1]

After Nebuchadnezzar defeated Egyptian and Assyrian forces, he conquered Jerusalem and deported many of Jerusalem's leaders. Since Daniel, Hananiah, Mishael and Azariah were deemed "youths without blemish…skillful in all wisdom…and competent to serve in the king's palace (Daniel 1:4 *RSVCE*)" they were deported to Babylon where they served in the king's court.

Both Judaism and Christianity have traditionally attributed the book to the young man Daniel. According to the first century A.D. Jewish historian Josephus, "for the several books that he [Daniel] wrote and left behind him

---

[1] Gordon J. McConville, *Exploring the Old Testament: A Guide to the Prophets: 4 Exploring the Bible Series* (Downers Grove: InterVarsity Press, 2002), 109.

are still read by us till this time; and from them we believe that Daniel conversed with God; for he did not only prophesy of future events, as did the other prophets, but he also determined the time of their accomplishment."[2] Many modern-day biblical scholars, however, writes Hahn:

> argue that the book was written under the name "Daniel" by an unknown Jewish author in the second century B.C., perhaps around 164. Proponents typically view the book as a response to the assault on Palestinian Judaism by the Seleucid ruler Antiochus IV Epiphanes, a crisis that reached its height between 167 and 164 B.C.[3]

These scholars claim that the prophecies in Daniel were written after what was prophesied took place.[4] However, as Bergsma and Pitre remark, this common view contrasts with "ancient Jewish and Christian tradition [which] unanimously understood the book of Daniel to be the composition of the Judean exile and prophet of the same name...[and] the narratives in the book of Daniel as history and the oracles as predictive of future events."[5]

The main languages of the prophetic literature are as follows: an introduction in Hebrew (Daniel 1-2:3), a body in Aramaic (Daniel 2:4-7:28), and a conclusion in Hebrew (Daniel 8-12). The conclusion is followed by two chapters in Greek. The first of the two is on Susanna (13:1-64), and the other is on Priests of Bel, a Dragon, and a Lion's Den (14:1-42). Chapter three also contains two sections in Greek: Prayer of Azariah and Song of the Three Men

---

[2] Josephus, "Antiquities of the Jews – Book X, Chapter 11," ccel.org, https://ccel.org/ccel/josephus/complete/complete.ii.xi.xi.html.

[3] Scott Hahn, and Curtis Mitch, *Daniel: Ignatius Catholic Study Bible: 16*, Kindle Edition (San Francisco: Ignatius Press, 2013), loc. 260-270.

[4] Hahn and Mitch, loc. 260-270.

[5] John Bergsma and Brant Pitre, *A Catholic Introduction to the Bible, Volume I* (San Francisco: Ignatius Press, 2018), Kindle Location 19240.

(3:1-68 in italics). These two concluding chapters are believed to be inspired writings by Catholics and Orthodox Christians but not by Judaism or Protestantism. Some scholars believe it that although Greek translations of the Old Testament contain these two chapters they were likely composed in Hebrew or in Aramaic.[6]

That the body of Daniel was first written in Aramaic is not debated. This Aramaic body reflects the international language at the time of the Babylonian exile since the common language of the Babylonian conquerors was Aramaic. This language and its alphabet were adopted by the Jewish people. Below is a chart that Michael Carasik uses to show in simple format the relationship of ancient Hebrew (Paleo Hebrew) with Aramaic and Biblical Hebrew. Paleo Hebrew used the Phoenician alphabet. Aramaic is based on the Phoenician alphabet with a number of modifications as is evident in the chart. At the time of the Babylonian exile, the Aramaic alphabet was adopted, and the Bible was written with Aramaic letters. Aramaic also become commonly spoken by the Jewish people as well, which helps to explain why the body of book of Daniel is written in Aramaic.

Besides the clear section divisions by language, the book is divided into two main sections. The first describes Daniel, Hananiah, Mishael, and

---

[6] Bergsma and Pitre, Kindle Location 19231.

[7] Michael Carasik, *Biblical Hebrew: Learning a Sacred Language* (Chantilly: The Teaching Company, 2018), accompanying video.

Azariah at service in the Babylonian Court (chapters 1-6). The second is Daniel's visions (chapters 7-12). This is followed by the two previously mentioned chapters.

Section Questions

1. What is the possible explanation that McConville provides for the apparent contradiction between how the book of Daniel dates the third year of King Jehoiakim's reign with the historical reference point of the 605 B.C. Battle of Carchemish?
2. What is the traditional understanding of who wrote Daniel and how, with respect to prophecy, and a dominant modern approach?
3. What are the three languages that the Book of Daniel was composed in?

At Service in the Babylonian Court Chapters 1-6

Chapter one depicts the Jewish royal youth, Daniel and his three companions, at service in King Nebuchadnezzar's court. At the court, they were given Babylonian names and educated in Babylonian ways. When it came to Babylonian food, the chief eunuch permitted Daniel, Hananiah, Mishael and Azariah to be faithful to Jewish dietary law as long their diet did not cause them to become malnourished (Daniel 1:15).

Since, Daniel and his three companions are faithful to Jewish purity laws and refuse to worship the false Gods of the Babylonians (Daniel 3:18) they are not condemned for serving in the court of a king who was responsible for destroying the holy city of Jerusalem and its temple. Instead, the text distinguishes, explains Bergsma and Pitre, between "civil service" to a lawful authority, which the Daniel and his companions did, and engaging in state sanctioned worship of false gods, which Daniel and his companions did not do.

As presented in the book, Daniel's and his three companions' civil service is praiseworthy since they maintained their Jewish identity by refusing to worship false Gods.[8] This lesson is particularly applicable for many in today's highly secular times, where civil governments often actively persecute Christians. Participation and even collaboration with modern day civil governments, even corrupt ones, can be morally upright as long as one's Christian identity is maintained in the midst of service to the government.

In chapter two, Daniel dutifully serves King Nebuchadnezzar by interpreting a disturbing dream the king had. The king imperiously orders that not only his dream be interpreted but also that the interpreter describe the dream without the king telling what the dream consisted of. Obeying the king, and listening to God as the true heavenly king, Daniel describes the dream of the king. In his dream, the king saw a terrifying image of a figure with a gold head, silver arms and breast, bronze belly and thighs, iron legs, and feet partly made up of iron and clay. A stone that was "cut out by no human hand" struck the feet of the figure and it broke into pieces that were carried away by wind.

Daniel interprets the dream as representing four consecutive kingdoms. As Richard J. Clifford explains the identity of these kingdoms is less important than that there are four kingdoms, four. Four, in ancient times was used to signify something that is universal such as evident in the phrase "four corners of the earth (Isaiah 11:12; Revelation 7:1)." This expression refers to the whole world in a similar sense as the reference to four kingdoms refer to all political kingdoms in history which ceaselessly replace one another. According to mythology, when one kingdom fell and was replaced by another, the god of the fallen kingdom also fell in prominence only to be replaced by another god.[9]

---

[8] Bergsma and Pitre, Kindle Location 19363.

[9] Fr. Richard J. Clifford, *Enjoying the Old Testament*, 9 CDs and Study Guide (Now You Know Media,).

The uncut stone that interrupts this cyclical nature of political history has traditionally been understood as a prophecy of Jesus who by being born of a Virgin is like a virginal stone that is uncut by human hands. Jesus then establishes an everlasting kingdom, a fifth kingdom (Daniel 2:44; 7:27), that due to its perfection will not be replaced by any other kingdom. As Gregory of Nyssa teaches, "What is the stone . . . but Christ? For of him Isaiah says, 'And I am laying in Zion for a foundation, a costly stone, precious, elect'; and Daniel likewise, 'A stone was cut out but not by hand,' that is, Christ was born without a man."[10] The growing of the stone into "a great mountain" that fills "the whole earth (Daniel 2:35 *RSVCE*)" is likewise interpreted as Christ's presence extended in time through his Church.

Augustine interprets a verse from psalm three where David cries "aloud to the Lord and he answers me from his holy mountain (Psalm 3:4 *RSVCE*)" as referring to Christ's "holy church. It is that mountain which, according to Daniel's vision, grew from a very small stone till it overtook the kingdoms of the earth and grew to such a size that it 'filled the face of the earth.'"[11] It will overtake all other kingdoms by breaking them "in pieces (Daniel 2:44 RSVCE)." As interpreted by Hahn and Mitch, Jesus proclaims that he is this stone prophesied by Daniel. "Everyone who falls on that stone will be broken to pieces; but when it falls on any one it will crush him (Luke 20:18 *RSVCE*)."[12]

In reference to Exodus (20:25) and the first book of Kings (6:7), which direct that sacred altars are to be made from uncut stone, Bergsma and Pitre

---

[10] Kenneth Stevenson and Michael Glerup, *Ancient Christian Commentary on Scripture: Old Testament XIII, Ezekiel, Daniel* (Downers Grove: IVP Academic: 2008), 347. Gregory of Nyssa's *On the Baptism of Christ* is cited.

[11] Stevenson and Glerup, 347. Augustine's *Explanations of the Psalms* 43.4 is cited.

[12] Hahn and Mitch, Kindle Location 1828-1834.

demonstrate that this stone not cut by hand which eventually fills the earth is intended to be understood as a temple around which all of the universe is properly ordered and centered upon since the temple represents God's Holy presence.[13] The belief that the Temple signifies God's presence who is the center of reality is directly applicable to our lives, as Bishop Barron explains: "When we find the center in God then every aspect of our self comes together coherently around that center. ... The trouble with sin is that we have lost our center, and therefore the elements that make us up become dispersed, disparate."[14] The ultimate centering temple is the Temple of Jesus Christ who invites all of us to be ordered around by being members of his body, where we harmoniously dwell with one another as we think through the mind of Jesus Christ and love with the same Heart of Jesus.

At the time of Jesus' birth, the Jewish people's hope for the fifth kingdom prophesied by Daniel was particularly intense. This is because, comments Bergsma and Pitre, a common interpretation of the four kingdoms was that the four kingdoms in chronological order were Babylon, Medo-Persia (which Daniel conceives as one kingdom - Daniel 5:28), Greece, and Rome. The first century B.C. non-canonical Jewish writing *The Psalms of Solomon* describe such a savior king who will bring in the fifth, everlasting kingdom:

> Behold, O Lord, and raise up unto them their king, the son of David.
> At the time in the which Thou seest, O God, that he may reign over
> Israel Thy servant. And gird him with strength, that he may shatter
> unrighteous rulers. And that he may purge Jerusalem from nations
> that trample (her) down to destruction. ... At his rebuke nations
> shall flee before him. And he shall reprove sinners for the thoughts
> of their heart. And he shall gather together a holy people, whom he

---

[13] Bergsma and Pitre, Kindle Location 18897.

[14] Robert Barron, *David the King*, (Word on Fire Catholic Ministries, 2017), DVD, Lesson Four, Gathered in Jerusalem.

shall lead in righteousness. And he shall judge the tribes of the people that has been sanctified by the Lord his God.… And he (shall be) a righteous king, taught of God, over them. All nations (shall be) in fear before him.[15]

The first century A.D. non-canonical Jewish book *2 Esdras* also contains a similar Messianic expectation:

My son the Messiah shall appear with his companions and bring four hundred years of happiness to all who survive. At the end of that time, my son the Messiah shall die, and so shall all mankind who draw breath. Then the world shall return to its original silence for seven days as at the beginning of creation, and no one shall be left alive.[16]

Other early first century B.C. and A.D. Jewish writings also contain expectations of the coming a Messiah. During this time of heightened hope for a Messiah under Roman rule, Jesus was born. He was born in a time when many were hoping that the fifth, perfect kingdom of God would bring an end to the cyclical nature of violently sinful kingdoms that Rome was but one of. Interestingly, some propose that Jesus' death on the cross in 33 A.D. coincides with the 490 years "seventy weeks of years (Daniel 9:24 *RSVCE*)"

---

[15] "Psalms of Solomon," wesley.nnu.edu, http://wesley.nnu.edu/sermons-essays-books/noncanonical-literature/noncanonical-literature-ot-pseudepigrapha/the-psalms-of-solomon/, Chapter 17, 23-38. The following is cited, Translated from Greek and Syriac manuscripts by G. Buchanan Gray in R. H. Charles, ed., The Apocrypha and Pseudepigrapha of the Old Testament in English (Oxford: Clarendon Press, 1913) 2: 631-652

[16] "4 Ezra (2 Esdras)," scribd.com, https://www.scribd.com/doc/2019085/4-Ezra-Revised-English, chapter 7, 28-31.

prophesied by Daniel for the coming of the fifth kingdom.[17] As presented by Pitre, the beginning of the 490 years may be interpreted as taking place in 457 B.C. when Artaxerxes the King of Persia decreed that the Temple be rebuilt. The rebuilding of Jerusalem (9:25 cf. Ezra 7:11-26) in chapter nine may be referring to this decree being enacted. 457 plus 33 neatly equals 490.[18] Needless to say, many Scripture scholars disagree with this interpretation especially those who maintain that the prophecies in Daniel are not prophecies of events that are to take place in the future but rather are "prophecies" written after events already have taken place.

Even though King Nebuchadnezzar "fell upon his face and did homage to Daniel (Daniel 2:46 *RSVCE*)" after Daniel correctly described and interpreted the king's dream, the king quickly turns on Daniel's three companions when they refuse to worship an idol. In anger, the king has them thrown into a "burning fiery furnace (Daniel 3:17 *RSVCE*)." In the furnace, the three "walked about in the midst of the flames, singing hymns to God and blessing the Lord (Daniel 3:1 *RSVCE*)." Surprised that they are unharmed, King Nebuchadnezzar looks into the furnace and sees someone walking with the three young men. This person looks "like a son of the gods (Daniel 3:25 *RSVCE*)." Church Fathers interpreted this mysterious figure as the Second Person of the Blessed Trinity, the Word of God prior to the Incarnation. Irenaeus writes:

> It is manifest [in Scripture] that the Father is indeed invisible, of whom also the Lord said, "No one has seen God at any time." But his Word, as he willed it and for the benefit of those who saw, did show the Father's brightness and explained his will. . . . He appeared

---

[17] Bergsma and Pitre, Kindle Location 18909. The following is also referenced, Daniel 6:8, 12, 15; 8:20.

[18] Brant Pitre, *The Old Testament-A Historical and Theological Journey through Jewish*, study outline.

to those who saw him not in one figure or in one character but according to the reasons and purposes that he wanted to achieve, as we see written in Daniel. He was seen with those who were around Ananias, Azarias and Misael as present with them in the furnace of fire, in the burning, and preserving them from [the effects of] fire: "And the appearance of the fourth," it is said, "was like the Son of God." At another time [he is represented as] "a stone cut out of the mountain without hands" and as destroying all temporal kingdoms . . . and as himself filling all the earth. Then too he is the same being beheld as the Son of man coming in the clouds of heaven and drawing near to the Ancient of Days.[19]

St. Jerome interprets the fourth man as foreshadowing Jesus who after dying on the cross descends into the Hell "not to destroy the hell of damnation, but to free the just who had gone before him."[20] "[T]his angel of the Son of God foreshadows our Lord Jesus Christ, who descended into the furnace of hell, in which the souls of both sinners and of the righteous are imprisoned, in order that he might without suffering any scorching by fire or injury to his person deliver those who were held imprisoned by chains of death."[21]

Focusing on the three young men themselves who courageously praised God in the midst of the flames to the astonishment of their pagan captors, Bergsma and Pitre comment that their actions accomplished the purpose of the Temple of Jerusalem that the Babylonians destroyed in 586 B.C.

---

[19] Stevenson and Glerup, 351. The following is cited, Irenaeus's *Against Heresies* 4.20.11.

[20] "Catechism of the Catholic Church," vatican.va, http://www.vatican.va/archive/ccc_css/archive/catechism/p122a5p1.htm, no. 633.

[21] Stevenson and Glerup, 352. The following is cited, Jerome's *Commentary on Daniel* 3.92 [25].

According to King Solomon's dedication prayer to God over the newly constructed Temple, the Temple's purpose is that "all peoples of the earth may know your name and fear you [God]... and that they may know that this house ... is called by your name (1 Kings 8:43 *RSVCE*)."[22]

In chapter four King Nebuchadnezzar has another disturbing dream of a massive tree that "was visible to the end of the whole earth (Daniel 4:11 *RSVCE*)" and provides shelter to all kinds of life. An angel appears who cuts down the tree. Daniel interprets the tree as representing the King who, unless he repents, will lose his mind and will be cut off from human interaction by being "driven from among men (Daniel 4:25 *RSVCE*). A way to regain what he loses is repentance. Repentance means "practicing righteousness, and ... by showing mercy to the oppressed (Daniel 4:27 *RSVCE*)." A year later the king lost his mind and was driven from his throne. When he regains his reason, Nebuchadnezzar repents of his evil ways, praises God and is reestablished on his throne. Like King Manasseh's repentance, Nebuchadnezzar change of heart and God's forgiveness of the king's evil ways is a message of hope in the possible repentance and transformation of the even the hardest of hearts.

Chapter five introduces another king, King Belshazzar, who is identified as Nebuchadnezzar's son. In an apparent contradiction, a clay cylinder that was found in 1854 A.D. in Ur, Iraq by J.E. Taylor, identifies King Belshazzar as the son of King Nabonidus (556-539 B.C.).[23] An explanation for this apparent contradiction, explain Bergsma and Pitre, is that the term father in Daniel 5:2 does not necessarily mean Belshazzar's biological father but rather could be referring to a dynastic father that Belshazzar claims as his father to legitimize his rule.[24] As he served Nebuchadnezzar, Daniel also served

---

[22] Bergsma and Pitre, Kindle Location 19373.

[23] Clyde E. Fant & Mitchell G. Reddish, *Lost Treasures of the Bible* (Grand Rapids: William B. Eerdmans Publishing Company, 2008), 232-233.

[24] Bergsma and Pitre, Kindle Location 18988.

Belshazzar. A way Daniel served the king is by interpreting the writing of a hand that mysteriously appears while the king is feasting with his court and drinking sacrilegiously from precious vessels that Nebuchadnezzar had confiscated from the Jerusalem Temple before destroying it.

"Immediately (Daniel 5:5 RSVCE)" after this reckless disregard for items associated with religious worship the hand writes words on a palace wall: "Mene, Mene, Tekel, and Parsin (Daniel 5:25 *RSVCE*)." Upon being brought in to interpret the writing, Daniel says "This is the interpretation of the matter: Mene, God has numbered the days of your kingdom and brought it to an end; Tekel, you have been weighed in the balances and found wanting; Peres, your kingdom is divided and given to the Medes and Persians (Daniel 5:28 *RSVCE*)." That same night the king is killed and is replaced by Darius the Mede. In c. 550 B.C., the Medes were conquered by the Persians under the leadership of Cyrus the Great and became incorporated into the Medo-Persian Empire which replaced the Babylonian empire of Nebuchadnezzar and Belshazzar.

Under Darius's rule, Daniel was promoted to be one of the "one hundred twenty satraps (Daniel 6:1 *RSVCE*)" who helped the king to rule his empire. Daniel governed so well that the king "planned to set him over the whole kingdom (Daniel 6:3 *RSVCE*)." This plan caused the other satraps to be envious and plot on how to eliminate Daniel. Their plot consisted in obtaining the king's signature on a decree that forbade for thirty days anyone in the Medo-Persian Empire from praying to any god or petitioning any man. When the decree went into effect, Daniel prayed to God discreetly in his room. Suspecting that Daniel was violating the decree, the plotters spied on Daniel and caught him praying. Faithful to his decree, the king ordered Daniel to be thrown into a lions' den. God, though, protected Daniel from being harmed by the lions. Seeing that Daniel was unharmed by the lions, the king ordered Daniel to be taken out of the den and the accusers to be cast in instead along with their immediate families.

Section Questions

1. Why, according to Bergsma and Pitre, are Daniel and his companions not condemned for serving in a pagan court ruled by a king who persecuted the Jewish people?

2. According to Clifford what does the number four represent in Daniel's vision of four kingdoms?

3. According to Church Fathers how does Jesus and the Church fulfill Daniel's vision of an uncut stone? Include in your response the following: altars, temple.

4. With respect to Daniel's prophesied fifth kingdom, at the time of Jesus what were many Jewish people hoping? Include the following in your response: *The Psalms of Solomon, 2 Esdras*, Messiah, 70 Weeks of Years.

5. How does Jerome interpret the fourth person who accompanies Daniel and companions during their time in a furnace?

6. How does Bergsma and Pitre explain the apparent contradiction between the historical clay cylinder artifact found in 1854 that identifies King Belshazzar as the son of King Nabonidus with Daniel 5:2 that identifies King Belshazzar as King Nebuchadnezzar's son?

7. How specifically does Daniel interpret the words *Mene, Tekel*, and *Peres* in Daniel 5:28?

8. How specifically do the other satraps respond to Daniel when they find out that King Darius is planning to set Daniel "over the whole kingdom (Daniel 6:3)?

Daniel's Visions Chapters 7-12

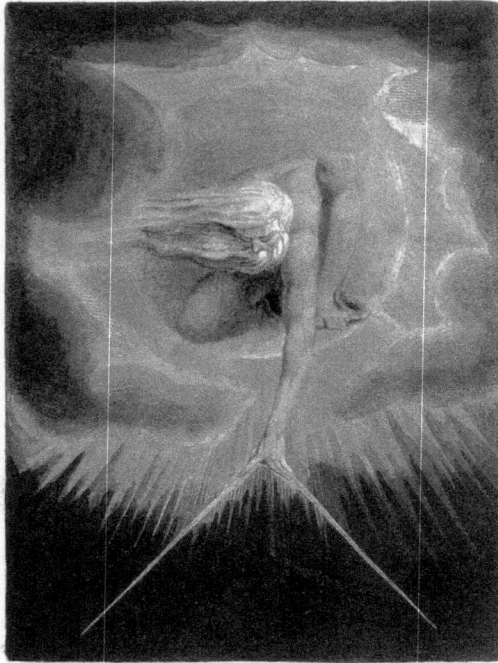

The second section of the book describes Daniel's visions. Chapter seven's vision of four beasts who emerge from the sea provide further details about the coming perfect fifth eternal kingdom referred to in chapter two. It will be established by a being coming on the "clouds of heaven" who looks "like a son of man," is presented "to the Ancient of Days" and is given "dominion and glory and kingdom" over all people (Daniel 7:13-14 *RSVCE*)." Clouds in the Old Testament often indicate the presence of God.

---

[25] William Blake / Public domain, "The Ancient of Days (1794) Watercolor etching by William Blake," https://commons.wikimedia.org/wiki/File:Europe_a_Prophecy,_copy_D,_object_1_(Bentley_1,_Erdman_i,_Keynes_i)_British_Museum.jpg.

God overshadows the tabernacle in the form of a cloud; a pillar of cloud leads the Israelites through the desert during the daytime hours (Exodus 13:21); and God tells Moses that he will appear in "in the cloud upon the mercy seat (Leviticus 16:2 *RSVCE*)" on the Day of Atonement.[26]

The being who descends on heavenly clouds looks "like a son of man (Daniel 7:13 *RSVCE*)" and will present himself before the "Ancient of Days". In other words, as Miller explains, someone who appears to be like human being will present himself before God who is ancient since God is "not bound by time."[27] The human like appearance of the presenter, coupled with his origin from heaven indicates that he is more than human. The ancient Jewish non-canonical religious writing, *The Book of Enoch* (300-200 B.C.), also known as 1 Enoch, interprets this mysterious person as follows:

> There I beheld the Ancient of days, whose head was like white wool, and with him another, whose countenance resembled that of man. His countenance was full of grace, like that of one of the holy angels. Then I inquired of one of the angels, who went with me, and who showed me every secret thing, concerning this Son of man; who he

---

[26] The connection of "coming on clouds" with a special revelation of God, Miller contends, likely originates outside of Israel. "The 'coming on the clouds' image is older than that, I believe, and this is something I've written on extensively. The biblical writers are drawing on a very old image here that comes out of Canaanite mythology. The central Canaanite myth is about the senior god El, an Ancient of Days, so to speak. We know this from tablets discovered at the ancient city Syrian city Ugarit, as well as from images in seals and art from Canaan. El eventually hands over his kingship to a younger god Baal, who is repeatedly called 'rider on the clouds.'" Robert D. Miller II, *Understanding the Old Testament* (Chantilly: The Teaching Company, 2019), 289.

[27] Miller, 288.

was; whence he was; and why he accompanied the Ancient of days.

2. He answered and said to me, This is the Son of man, to whom righteousness belongs; with whom righteousness has dwelt; and who will reveal all the treasures of that which is concealed: for the Lord of spirits has chosen him; and his portion has surpassed all before the Lord of spirits in everlasting uprightness.

3. This Son of man, whom thou beholdest, shall raise up kings and the mighty from their couches, and the powerful from their thrones; shall loosen the bridles of the powerful, and break in pieces the teeth of sinners.[28] ...

2. In that hour was this Son of man invoked before the Lord of spirits, and his name in the presence of the Ancient of days.

3. Before the sun and the signs were created, before the stars of heaven were formed, his name was invoked in the presence of the Lord of spirits. A support shall he be for the righteous and the holy to lean upon, without falling; and he shall be the light of nations.[29]

With these words, the *Book of Enoch* claims, writes Miller, that "the Son of Man enthroned by God before the creation of the world is the messiah."[30] According to Christianity, as represented by Justin Martyr, this Messianic prophecy was fulfilled by the Incarnation of Jesus, born of a Virgin:

---

[28] "The Book of Enoch," book-ofenoch.com, http://book-ofenoch.com/chapter-46/, chapter 46.

[29] "The Book of Enoch," chapter 48.

[30] Miller, 290.

Does not Daniel allude to this very truth when he says that he who received the eternal kingdom is "as a Son of man"? The words "as a Son of man" indicate that he would become man and appear as such but that he would not be born of a human seed. Daniel states the same truth figuratively when he call Christ "a stone cut out without hands," for, to affirm that he was cut out without hands signifies that he was not the product of human activity but of the will of God, the Father of all, who brought him forth.[31]

In contrast to the divine being who descends on heavenly clouds, four beasts rise up from the depth of the sea, a place associated in the Bible with evil, violence, and disorder. When Isaiah speaks of the day of judgment and redemption he describes an evil dragon called Leviathan who dwells in the chaotic, destructive waters of the sea: "In that day the Lord with his hard and great and strong sword will punish Leviathan the fleeing serpent, Leviathan the twisting serpent, and he will slay the dragon (*nachash* נָחָשׁ) that is in the sea (Isaiah 27:1 *RSVCE*)." Isaiah also call the dragon from the sea Rahab: "Awake, awake, put on strength, O arm of the Lord…Was it not you who cut Rahab in pieces, who pierced the dragon (*tannin* תַּנִּין)? (Isaiah 51:9 *RSVCE*)"

This dragon, as interpreted by Robert D. Miller, is the serpent (Genesis 3:13 *nachash* נָחָשׁ) who tempts Adam and Eve in Genesis. He explains, "the serpent there is not a snake. It doesn't crawl on the ground until the end of the story. And a serpent that doesn't go on the ground is by nature a dragon."[32] As Daniel and other books in the Bible repeat multiple times, the

---

[31] Stevenson and Glerup, 378. The following is cited, Justin Martyr *Dialogue with Trypho* 76.

[32] Miller, 383. According to Miller the dragon image likely came from outside of Israel. "[T]he biblical writers took this image from a narrative story known to their neighbors, the Canaanites, who proceeded the Israelites in the Promised Land and continued to be their closest neighbors throughout

the early history. We know Canaanite mythology from texts discovered by archaeologists at the site of ancient Ugarit on the Syrian coast. These Ugaritic texts originated in the 15th through 13th centuries BCE. Now, that's quite a bit earlier than the time of ancient Israel and encompasses an area quite a bit further north. But we know that the myths presented in those texts survived among Canaanite people centuries later, and much further south. Proof of this are iconographic images depicting those stories that have been found archaeologically in ancient Israel. The most important specific story here is the myth of the god Baal. The Canaanites' religion had a pantheon of gods on the model of a family. There is the senior high god, El, along with his wife and children: Yamm, Anat, and Baal. ... There is a further myth (preserved poorly) in which Hedammu—who has the form of a serpent—comes forth from the sea and undermines the rule of the king of heaven by wreaking havoc on earth before being destroyed by Teshub. In both cases, the storm god needs his sister's help. But, that myth, too, was borrowed; in this case from the Hittites who lived in ancient Turkey. From 1600 BCE, we have the Hittite Illuyanka myth. Their storm and agriculture god, Tarhuna, fights the dragon Illuyanka. The storm god initially loses. The battle is set at the sea, and Illuyanka is called 'Illuyanka of the sea.' Victory comes only with the help of a sister goddess and some trickery. And the victory is followed by a banquet assembly of gods. The myth was narrated yearly in a New Year's festival, and it reinforced the role of the human king. Now, if this couldn't get any weirder, the Hittites had an Indo-European language, related not to Hebrew or Canaanite but to Latin, Greek and Russian, and also to Sanskrit, the ancient language of India. And there is a nearly identical myth in the Hindu Rigveda, from the 16th century BCE, about the storm god Indra. All the elements are there again: a storm god who is an agricultural god; a dragon from the sea named Vritra; other gods who cower in fear; an initial defeat of the storm god; special weapons that bring victory; a mountain feast; enthronement as king of gods; implications for the human king; and a New

sea monsters, (in the form of four beasts, Leviathan and Rahab) will be completely defeated by God acting patiently through history. All evil creatures (dragon, beast from the sea, beast from the earth) will be completely vanquished by the blood of Christ (Revelation 12-22), and will receive final judgment by Jesus when returns as judge (Revelation 20:11-15).

Chapter eight contains Daniel's second vision. In this vision Daniel sees a ram with two horns which clashes with a fierce he-goat. The goat overcomes the ram and tramples upon the ram victoriously. The goat, though, loses his horn that helped him to defeat the ram. In its place grow four horns. From one of these four horns grows a horn that grows into a huge horn. In Angel Gabriel's explanation of the dream to Daniel, the ram with two horns represents the Medo-Persian empire. This empire was defeated by the Greek empire, represented by the he-goat whose destructive horn symbolizes Alexander the Great.

The falling off of the goat's horn signifies Alexander's death who left behind an empire divided four ways between his four top generals. The four horns on the goat's head represent these four generals and their four territories. The horn that sprouts a little horn is most likely, comment Bergsma and Pitre, a symbol of the Seleucid Empire and the little horn that grows into a massive size is the Seleucid King Antiochus IV Epiphanes who was responsible for severely persecuting the Jewish people. Antiochus sacked the Jerusalem temple, prohibited the practice of Judaism, and dedicated an altar in the Temple to Zeus (2 Maccabees 6:1-12).[33]

Unlike his preceding visions, chapter nine's vision comes to Daniel not while he is sleeping but when he is engaged in prayer to God. As Daniel prays and begs God for mercy, God tells Daniel "Seventy weeks of years are decreed

---

Year's recitation. And even the words of the Rigveda are related to those in Illuyanka." Robert D. Miller II, *Understanding the Old Testament* (Chantilly: The Teaching Company, 2019), 375-377.

[33] Bergsma and Pitre, Kindle Location 19124.

concerning your people and your holy city, to finish the transgression, to put an end to sin, and to atone for iniquity (Daniel 9:24 *RSVCE*)." Seventy years times seven years is four hundred and ninety years. Church Fathers interpreted this prophecy as fulfilled in Christ. Ishodad of Merv explains, "Seventy weeks make 490 years; they are calculated from the time when they will come back from Babylon and will begin to build the temple to the year when the Romans will make war against them after the ascension of our Lord."[34]

Chapters ten through twelve contain Daniel's last visions. Chapter ten describes a heavenly being who resembles a man. This messenger of God contends with evil princes, specifically again the "prince of Persia" and the "prince of Greece (Daniel 10:20 *RSVCE*)." "There is none who contends by my side," the messenger says, "except Michael, your prince (Daniel 10:21 *RSVCE*)." Church Fathers interpreted these three princes as spiritual powers, fallen angelic beings, that rule behind the thrones. The spiritual power that influences the throne of the Persians and Greeks are diabolical powers. Along with these evil spiritual intelligences, the fallen angels, comments Ammonius of Alexandria, are guardian angels appointed by God for every nation "so that they may not be harmed by the demons."[35] The purely spiritual intelligence, the angel that God appointed over Israel is Michael the Archangel.[36]

In chapter eleven, an angel shows Daniel a vision of a final battle among the nations. In the midst of this world war, the archangel Michael appears again: "At that time shall arise Michael, the great prince who has charge of

---

[34] Stevenson and Glerup, Kindle Location 10081 of 19343. The following is cited, Isho'dad of Merv's *Commentary on Daniel* 9.24.

[35] Stevenson and Glerup, Kindle Location 10569 of 19343. The following is cited, Ammonius of Alexandria's *Fragments on Daniel* 10.20.

[36] Stevenson and Glerup, Kindle Location 10475 of 19343. The following is cited, Theodoret of Cyr *Commentary on Daniel* 10.13.

your people (Daniel 12:1 *RSVCE*)." Michael will oversee the very end of times when "many of those who sleep in the dust of the earth shall awake, some to everlasting life, and some to shame and everlasting contempt (Daniel 12:2 *RSVCE*)."

Section Questions

1. In Daniel's chapter seven vision, who initiates the fifth kingdom and what is this person's identity? Include the following in your response: Clouds, Ancient of Days, *The Book of Enoch*

2. According to Miller, how are the four beasts who emerge from the sea in Daniel chapter seven related to the serpent in Genesis chapter three?

3. According to the angel Gabriel what does the following symbolize in Daniel's chapter eight vision: He-Goat, Ram, Horns

4. What is the role of the angel Michael in chapters ten and eleven of Daniel? Include in your response the following: Evil Princes, National Guardian, Nations, Angels

Susanna, Bel, Dragon, and Lion's Den Chapters 13-14

Chapters thirteen and fourteen contain stories about Daniel's divinely given courage. In the first story, Daniel, as a young child, boldly defends the innocent life of the virtuous woman Susanna who is falsely accused of sexual sin by two lustful elders. Heeding Daniel's questioning of the elders, which revealed Susanna's innocence and the elders' guilt, the assembled people put the two elders to death: "Thus innocent blood was saved that day (Daniel 13:62 *RSVCE*)."

The following chapter describes Daniel defeating the priests of Bel and slaying a dragon. The chapter begins with the Persian King Cyrus asking

Daniel why he did not worship the God Bel whom the king worshipped. Daniel says that he only worships the true God of Israel who is living unlike the false God Bel. This response angers the king who swears that unless Daniel proves that Bel is not eating the food that is placed in Bel's temple then Daniel will die. Daniel cleverly demonstrates to the king that the priests of Bel and their families are eating the food placed before an idol of Bel, as evident by the footsteps they unwittingly leave behind at night-time after Daniel had strewn the temple's floor with ashes. Instead of putting Daniel to death, the king puts the priests to death and destroys the temple.

In destroying the temple, the king was destroying the false worship and false God that his society had been ordered around. This destruction of idolatry is in accordance with Daniel's God given mission is to foster true worship around the true, living God. Daniel's faith, as supported by his experience, taught him that societal unity around a false God is always

---

[37] Rembrandt / Public domain, "Susanna and the Elders, 1647," https://commons.wikimedia.org/wiki/File:Rembrandt_-_Susanna_and_the_Elders_-_WGA19104.jpg.

ephemeral and will pass, often violently. Due to false worship, Bishop Barron observes, Daniel's beloved kingdom of Judah entered into a civil war with Israel. In this weakened, divided state, nations organized around false gods easily conquered the Israelites and Judeans.[38]

As a prophet, Daniel is to live out the mission intended by God for Israel, as Bishop Barron phrases it, "to worship God a right, to be the new Eden." For when Israel does so "they would draw the rest of the world into right praise of God"[40] and as a result of the common worship around the one true, living God there will be peace, love, and unity among nations. If this does not happen, the worship of false Gods will continue to spawn violent competition among worldly powers, division, and hatred of neighbor in a never satisfying striving to be filled with what the natural, finite world offers.

---

[38] Robert Barron, *Priest, Prophet, King* (Word on Fire Catholic Ministries, 2017), Lesson Five, Ordering the Kingdom.

[39] After Guido Reni / Public domain, "Susanna and the Elders, by Guido Reni," https://commons.wikimedia.org/wiki/File:Guido_Reni_-_Susanna_and_the_Elders_-_WGA19296.jpg.

[40] Barron, Lesson Five, Ordering the Kingdom.

Only the worship and love of the infinite, living God can satisfy our hearts created for infinite love, which no amount of created reality ever can satisfy, whether it comes in the form of gold, power, bodily pleasure, or worldly recognition. All of created reality, preaches Barron echoing John Paul II's theology of the gift, is intended by God to be understood as gifts of love from the divine love giver.[41]

The gifts of created reality are not to be mistaken for the lover Himself, who is God. Otherwise, false worship will result based on the false expectation that the gift will satisfy our hearts when in reality only the giver of the gift, God, can satisfy our hearts. Daniel's role, as with all true prophets, is to uncover false worship that promises happiness, communion, and unity but always disappoints and leads to ever greater fragmentation, strife, and disunity as people fight over the limited goods of this earth with the false hope that the person who is able to have the most will be the happiest.

In contrast to this assumption of what will bring happiness, the Catholic faith teaches that happiness comes about precisely not by seeking to fill ourselves with the goods of this world but rather by giving ourselves away as a gift. The greatest expression of this blessed state is Jesus who gives himself totally to his heavenly Father in the love of the Holy Spirit, on the Cross, and in the Eucharist by giving us His body and blood. The reason that happiness for human beings comes about by giving ourselves away is because we are created in the image and likeness of a Triune God who is essentially a relational reality where, as St. Augustine explains, the Father loves the Son, the Son loves the Father and the mutual love is the Holy Spirit.[42] We only will experience peace when we live in accordance with this relational identity and likewise mutually give ourselves away in love. John Paul II called this the "law of the gift" which as Cardinal Avery Dulles comments was inspired by

---

[41] Barron, Lesson Five, Ordering the Kingdom.

[42] Augustine, "On the Trinity," newadvent.org, http://www.newadvent.org/fathers/130115.htm. book XV, chapter 17, no. 27.

Vatican II's teaching: "This likeness reveals that man, who is the only creature on earth which God willed for itself, cannot fully find himself except through a sincere gift of himself (*GS* 24)."[43]

In the final section of chapter fourteen Daniel slays a dragon. The dragon, as explained previously, stands for evil angelic powers that spreads chaos, division, and hatred, even though at times they promise precisely the opposite by enticing potential followers to become addicted on disordered love, love ordered to the goods of this world and not ultimately to God. In anger for having slain the dragon, the Babylonians throw Daniel in a lion's den. Once again, God intervenes, protects Daniel from the lions, and sends the prophet Habakkuk who gives Daniel food. Astonished, the king has Daniel pulled out the lions' den and orders the men who had plotted to

---

[43] "Gaudium et Spes, no. 24," vatican.va, http://www.vatican.va/archive/hist_councils/ii_vatican_council/documents/vat-ii_cons_19651207_gaudium-et-spes_en.html. Avery Cardinal Dulles, "John Paul II and the Truth About Freedom, August 1995," firstthings.com, https://www.firstthings.com/article/1995/08/004-john-paul-ii-and-the-truth-about-freedom.

[44] After Briton Rivière / Public domain, "published by Thomas Agnew and Sons, 1892 (*Daniel in the Lions' Den*)," https://commons.wikimedia.org/wiki/File:Daniellion.jpg.

destroy Daniel to be thrown in.

Section Questions

1. What does Daniel do that convinces the king that Bel is a false God?

The Twelve Minor Prophets

The Twelve Minor Prophets

Traditionally, the twelve minor prophets are ordered primarily chronologically. With the possible exception of Obadiah and Joel, whose dates are debated, the earlier prophets are placed first, and the later prophets are placed at the end. As Pitre and Bergsma present it, Hosea, Amos, Jonah, and Micah come first since they preached in the eighth century B.C. Next, comes Nahum, Habakkuk, and Zephaniah, who all lived in the seventh century. They are followed by Haggai, and Zechariah who lived in the sixth century B.C. Finally, the fifth century B.C. prophet Malachi comes last.[1]

Section Questions

1. Explain how chronologically the 12 Minor Prophets are ordered in a Catholic bible and provide the names for the first and last.

1. Hosea

According to the first verse of the book, Hosea, received the gift of prophecy during reign of the northern King of Israel Jeroboam II (c. r. 786-746 B.C.), the son of King Jo'ash (Jehoash).[2] Although, no place is directly

---

[1] John Bergsma and Brant Pitre, *A Catholic Introduction to the Bible, Volume I* (San Francisco: Ignatius Press, 2018), Kindle Location 19533.

[2] D.N. Freedman, *The Anchor Yale Bible Dictionary Vol. 3*, (New York: Doubleday, 1992), 745.

identified in the text as the birthplace of Hosea, it is the consensus of Biblical scholars that Hosea prophesied in the northern Kingdom of Israel.[3] Unlike Hosea, the rest of the twelve minor prophets, with the possible exception of Jonah, but this is disputed,[4] are from the southern Kingdom of Judah. The northern King Jeroboam II's last part of his reign, which Hosea lived in, coincides with the reign of King Azariah, the southern king of Judah, whose name is also mentioned in the first verse, along with three subsequent southern kings: Jotham, Ahaz, and Hezekiah (c. 715-687 B.C).[5] During King Hezekiah's reign, the northern King of Israel (2 Kings 18:9-10) fell to the Assyrian Empire (2 Kings 18:9-10) in circa 722 B.C. and never was restored.

The first chapter begins by describing the marital love between God and His bride Israel. In this chapter, God tells Hosea to marry the prostitute Gomer to signify Israel's infidelity to her divine spouse. In the following chapter, God promises that one day Israel will repent of her infidelity to her divine spouse and God speaking "tenderly to her (Hosea 2:14 *RSVCE*)" and "will espouse you forever; I will espouse you in righteousness and in justice, in steadfast love, and in mercy (Hosea 2:19 *RSVCE*)."

In this espousal, there will be a new "covenant" that will be established with all of creation "the beasts of the field, the birds of the air, and the creeping things of the ground; and I will abolish the bow, the sword, and war from the land (Hosea 2:18 *RSVCE*)." Since in Hebrew, the word bow is the same word for rainbow (קֶשֶׁת, *qesheth*),[6] the abolishing of the bow, comments Bergsma and Pitre, is an indirect reference to the God's covenant with Noah

---

[3] Freedman, 293.

[4] Carolyn Osiek, Leslie J. Hoppe, *Anselm Academic Study Bible: New American Bible Revised Edition* (Winona: Anselm Academic, 2013), 1474. "It is difficult to date but almost certainly post-exilic and may reflect the somewhat narrow, nationalistic reforms of Ezra and Nehemiah."

[5] Freedman, 753.

[6] Strong's Concordance, "7198. Qesheth," biblehub.com, http://biblehub.com/hebrew/7198.htm.

whose sign was a rainbow that God set in the sky as "a sign of the covenant between men and the earth (Genesis 9:13 *RSVCE*)." The hanging up of this bow writes, Hahn, has been interpreted as "a sign that God will no longer make war against humanity: God hangs us his war bow and retires it from service."[7]

The verse that follows verse 2:18 contains a number of Hebrew words whose definitions help to shed light on how God loves his people. The verse reads "And I will espouse you forever; I will espouse you in righteousness

---

[7] Scott Hahn, *Catholic Bible Dictionary* (New York: Doubleday, 2009), 126.

[8] James Tissot / Public domain, "Пророк Осия (The Prophet Hosea)," https://commons.wikimedia.org/wiki/File:%D0%9E%D1%81%D0%B8%D1%8F.jpg.

(*sedeq* צֶדֶק) and in justice (*mishpat* מִשְׁפָּט), in steadfast love (*hesed* (חֶסֶד), and in mercy (*rahamim* (רַחֲמִים) Hosea 2:19 *RSVCE*)."[9] The first two terms indicate that God's marital, covenantal love is righteous and just, especially in the sense of judging perfectly. These divine attributes related to justice are perfectly reconciled with love and mercy, or in the words of Pope Francis these seemingly diverse realities are "reconciled" as one.[10] As explained by Austen Ivereigh, this insight of Francis builds upon the reflection of Henri de Lubac on Trinitarian love present in the Catholic Church, "a *complexio oppositorum*, a system that synthesized elements that ordinarily pull in opposite directions, creating—through the power of the Holy Spirit—a unity out of diversity that respected difference."[11] The last of the attributes, mercy (*rahamim* רַחֲמִים), is of particular interest, since it is based on the Hebrew root *rechem* (רֶחֶם), meaning womb.[12] In Hebrew, being merciful literally means being a womblike person. In the bible, *rahamim* is applied to God and by so doing God's love is described in feminine terms. As Benedict XVI explains:

> The mystery of God's maternal love is expressed with particular power in the Hebrew word *rahamim*. Etymologically, this word means "womb," but it was later used to mean divine compassion for man, God's mercy. The Old Testament constantly uses the names of

[9] "6664. Tsedeq," biblehub.com, https://biblehub.com/hebrew/6664.htm.

[10] Francis, "Reconciled Diversity," ewtn.com, https://www.ewtn.com/catholicism/library/reconciled-diversity-13103.

[11] Austen Ivereigh, *Wounded Shepherd: Pope Francis and His Struggle to Convert the Catholic Church* (New York: Henry Holt and Company, 2019), 18.

[12] "7358. rechem," biblehub.com, https://biblehub.com/hebrew/7358.htm.

organs of the human body to describe basic human attitudes or inner dispositions of God, just as today we use *heart* or *brain* when referring to some aspect of our own existence. ... In this way the Old Testament portrays the basic attitudes of our existence, not with abstract concepts, but in the image language of the body. The womb is the most concrete expression for the intimate interrelatedness of two lives and of loving concern for the dependent, helpless creature whose whole being, body and soul, nestles in the mother's womb.[13]

Chapter three and four contrasts God's faithful, steadfast love with Israel's wavering, unfaithful love. Israel love, therefore, is likened to an adulteress and a prostitute. This comparison is particular valid, for at the time some in Israel were engaging in sexual relations with cultic prostitutes who waited outside of temples to false gods. It was believed that through sex with a temple prostitute union with the god of the temple would be achieved. Hosea presents worship of the true God of Israel as directly undermined by these false forms of worship. In addition, the worship of false gods, Barron comments, caused Israel to splinter into factions, and disintegrate. In its weakened state, powerful foreign empires invaded, conquered, and further disintegrated Israel through multiple deportations.[14] Hosea prophecies on the breakup of Israel concern the first invasion of the Assyrian Empire in 722 B.C. and subsequent deportation of Israel and its tribes.

In the following chapter, Hosea prophecies that the Kingdom of Judah will also one day suffer the same fate: "Ephraim [a term for the Kingdom of Israel] shall stumble in his guilt; Judah also shall stumble with them (Hosea

---

[13] Pope Benedict XVI, *Jesus of Nazareth, From the Baptism in the Jordan to the Transfiguration,* trans. Adrian J. Walker (New York: Double Day, 2007), Kindle location 2106 of 5265.

[14] Robert Barron, *Priest, Prophet, King,* (Word on Fire Catholic Ministries, 2017), Lesson Five, Ordering the Kingdom.

5:5 *RSVCE*).'" In 586 B.C., the Babylonian Empire conquered the Kingdom of Judah and, in a similar way to the Assyrian treatment of Israel, deported Judeans. Hosea then, in chapter six, prophecies that all is not lost for "on the third day he will raise us up (Hosea 6:2 *RSVCE*)." This expression of rising on the third day likely, comment McConville, is influenced by surrounding pagan cultures which worshiped a god who it was believed rose from the dead after three days.[15] Church Fathers interpreted this verse as fulfilled in Jesus Christ. Augustine writes, "Further on, Hosea foretold the resurrection of Christ on the third day, but in the mysterious way that is proper to prophecy. He says, 'He shall heal us after two days, and on the third day we shall rise again.'"[16] By rising from the dead, Jesus fulfilled this prophecy and the confused longings of pagans in their worship for such a rising from the dead, where life proves to be more powerful than death.

Christ's sacrificial death on the cross where He offered his life for our sake so that we may be mercifully spared punishment and restored to grace is a fulfillment of a verse that is also in chapter six: "I desire mercy and not sacrifice, the knowledge of God, rather than burnt offerings (Hosea 6:6 *RSVCE*)." In commenting on this verse, Amy Jill Levine writes, "Now, when the prophets here complain against the cult, they are not actually saying, in fact, get rid of the cult. This type of hyperbole is a standard form of ancient rhetoric, both Near Eastern in general and Hebrew rhetoric in particular. What the prophets will do is say, 'I want this instead of that,' but what they

---

[15] Gordon J. McConville, *Exploring the Old Testament: A Guide to the Prophets: 4 Exploring the Bible Series* (Downers Grove: InterVarsity Press, 2002), 142.

[16] Alberto Ferreiro, *Ancient Christian Commentary on Scripture, Old Testament XIV, The Twelve Prophets* (Downers Grove: InterVarsity Press, 2003), 62.

are really doing is saying, 'This is more important than that.'[17] On the cross, Jesus perfectly reconciled both sacrifice with mercy in way that was infinitely pleasing and which prioritized mercy over sacrifice since mercy is the reason and goal of Jesus' sacrifice on the Cross. The redemption that God desires to give to Israel but does not since "they speak lies against me (Hosea 7:13 RSVCE)" is achieved through Christ who came "into the world, to bear witness to the truth (John 18:37 RSVCE)." Christ's sacrificial death on the cross out of merciful love for sinners is the fullest interpretation of this verse from Hosea as Jesus taught after he was criticized for eating with public sinners: "Go and learn what this means, 'I desire mercy, and not sacrifice.' For I came not to call the righteous, but sinners (Matthew 9:13 RSVCE)."

In chapters eight, nine and ten, Hosea prophecies against Israel's sins of apostasy which Hosea likens to adultery and harlotry. Hosea also warns Israel of their coming punishment where God "will cast them off, because they have not listened to him; they shall be wanderers among the nations (Hosea 9:17 RSVCE)."

These warnings are immediately followed in chapter eleven with God assuring Israel of His love and reminding Israel of His mercy towards them in the past when they were in exile in Egypt: "When Israel was a child, I loved him, and out of Egypt I called my son (Hosea 11:1 RSVCE)." As McConville observes, the justice of God, in punishing Israel, and the mercy of God, in repeatedly rescuing Israel from punishment, distinguishes the true God of Israel from the many false Gods of the pagan nations where justice is attributed to one God, and mercy to another.[18]

---

[17] Amy-Jill Levine, *The Old Testament* (Chantilly: The Teaching Company, 2001), 310.

[18] Gordon J. McConville, *Exploring the Old Testament: A Guide to the Prophets: 4 Exploring the Bible Series* (Downers Grove: InterVarsity Press, 2002), 146. "A final implication of Hosea's belief in one God is that judgement and love are held together in tension (Emmerson 1984, p. 16).

The last three chapters testify to the true God in whom mercy and justice are united for God is the fullness of truth and not a part of the truth, not only part of reality. Chapter twelve emphasizes Israel's history of sinfulness. This is followed by chapter thirteen where God presents Himself as one who both judges and one who saves. Finally, in the last chapter, fourteen, God assures Israel that despite its sinfulness, despite the repeated punishments God has allowed to befall Israel, "I will heal their faithfulness; I will love them freely, for my anger has turned from them (Hosea 14:4 *RSVCE*)."

Section Questions

1. Who specifically did God tell Hosea to marry and why?
2. What is the meaning of the root word that the Hebrew word for mercy, *rahamim* רַחֲמִים is based on and how does this root word inform the Biblical understanding of mercy?
3. Hosea describes God as righteous, just, loving, and merciful. How is this description of God's characteristics different from how surrounding pagan nations described divine reality? Include in your response the following: Gods, Unity out of Diversity, Reconciled Diversity.
4. In Hosea, God says "I desire mercy and not sacrifice, the knowledge of God, rather than burnt offerings (Hosea 6:6 *RSVCE*)." How does Levine interpret this verse?

This is one of the great paradoxes of the Old Testament. It is true of the flood-story of Genesis 6—9, where one God brings the flood in judgement on humanity and saves humanity from the same flood by sparing Noah and his family. This is in contrast to the flood-stories of the Ancient Near East where these different acts are attributed to different gods (the god Enki, who favors Atrahasis (the 'Noah' figure), and protects him from the flood that is brought about by the god Ellil."

2. Joel

The book of Joel consists of only three chapters. The first chapter is a lament on the devastation wrought by "swarming" "hopping" and "destroying locusts (Hosea 1:4 *RSVCE*)." The remaining two chapters are on Judgment Day, when "[t]he sun shall be turned to darkness, and the moon to blood before the great and awesome day of the Lord comes (2:31 *RSVCE*)." The main message of Joel is to repent before it is too late, before days of judgment fall upon us. "For the day of the Lord is great and very awesome; who can endure it? 'Yet even now,' says the Lord, 'return to me with all your heart, with fasting, with weeping, and with mourning.... Return to the Lord, your God, for he is gracious and merciful (Joel 2:12-13 *RSVCE*)."

[19] James Tissot (1836-1902), French painter / Public domain, "Joel (watercolor circa 1896-1902 by James Tissot)," https://commons. wikimedia.org/wiki/File:Tissot_Joel.jpg.

The terrifying day of judgment will occur during the final battle of the nations in the "valley of Jehoshaphat (Joel 3:2 *RSVCE*)." The Hebrew word Jehoshapat (*Yehoshaphat*) is made up by two words, God (יְהֹוָה YHWH), and the root word for judging (שָׁפַט *shaphat*).[20] The valley's name literally means the place where God judges. According to Joel, God will fulfill the name of the valley of Jehoshaphat on Judgment Day. After God pronounces judgment and is, consequently, victorious over the nations, a time will come of true worship of God where a faithful remnant will rejoice and have plenty to eat. During this time, God promises, "my people shall never again be put shame…And it shall come to pass afterward, that I will pour out my spirit on all flesh (Joel 2:28 *RSVCE*)."

Church Fathers interpreted this prophecy as fulfilled by the sending of the Holy Spirit upon the Mary at the Annunciation (Ambrose), and by Jesus breathing upon his disciples saying, "Receive the Holy Spirit. If you forgive the sins of the any, they are forgiven; if you retain the sins of any, they are retained (John 20:22-23 *RSVCE*)"; and by the Holy Spirit descending at Pentecost (Theodore of Mopsuestia).[21]

Section Questions

1. According to Joel, where will the final battle of the nations take place, what will happen at the end of the battle, and how does the Hebrew name of where this battle takes place indicates what will happen at the end of the battle?

2. According to Church Fathers, when specifically was Joel's prophecy

---

[20] "3092. Yehoshaphat," biblehub.com, https://biblehub.com/hebrew/3092.htm.

[21] Ferreiro, 139-152. The following works are cited: Ambrose, *On the Holy Spirit* 1.7.85, Novatian, *On the Trinity* 29; Theodore of Mopsuestia, *Commentary on Joel* 2,28-32.

of the God pouring out his "spirit on all flesh (Joel 2:28)" fulfilled?

3. Amos

Introduction (1:1-2)

The nine chapters of Amos can be divided into five sections: Introduction (Amos 1:1-2), Oracles (Amos 1:3-2:16), Judgments (Amos 3:1-5:6), Woes and Warnings (Amos 5:7-6:14), Visions (Amos 7:1-9:15).[23]

---

[22] James Tissot (1836-1902), "Amos, circa 1896–1902, by James Jacques Joseph Tissot (French, 1836-1902)" https://commons.wikimedia.org/wiki/File:Tissot_Amos.jpg.

[23] D. Bergant, and R.J. Karris, *The Collegeville Bible Commentary: Based on the New American Bible with Revised New Testament* (Collegeville: Liturgical Press, 1989), 489-494; John Bergsma and Brant Pitre, *A Catholic*

The first verse identifies Amos as "among the shepherds of Tekoa (Amos 1:1 *RSVCE*)." A more literal translation is Amos was "among the sheep breeders." This translation is more literal than the *RSVCE* translation because the Hebrew word *noqed* (נֹקֵד) is used, which in 2 Kings 3:4 the *RSVCE* translates as sheep breeder and not simply as shepherd: "Mesha king of Moab was a sheep breeder." The distinction between shepherd and sheep breeder is important, argues Miller because a sheep breeder has significant higher social status than a shepherd. He writes, "If your translation says 'shepherd' it's not quite right. This is an owner of the flock, not the person who takes the livestock into the field. Amos is not a country bumpkin come to preach truth to power in the major cities. Amos was himself a wealthy landowner."[24]

Amos's high social status is indicated later in chapter seven which informs that Amos was a "dresser of sycamore trees (Amos 7:14 *RSVCE*)." Since, deduces Miller, sycamore trees "did not grow around Tekoa" the hometown of Amos, this means that Amos was a wealthy land owner who owned property apart from Tekoa, a town in the southern Kingdom of Judah.[25] Despite being from the southern kingdom, Amos's prophecies are directed to the northern Kingdom of Israel during the 8th century B.C. Amos began preaching to the northern kingdom "in the days of Uzziah king of Judah and in the days of Jeroboam to the son of Joash, king of Israel, two years before the earthquake (Amos 1:1 *RSVCE*)." Bergsma and Pitre comment that according to archaeologists this earthquake occurred c. 760 B.C.[26]

Introduction to the Bible, Volume I (San Francisco: Ignatius Press, 2018), Kindle Location 19717.

[24] Robert D. Miller II, *Understanding the Old Testament* (Chantilly: The Teaching Company, 2019), 242.

[25] Miller II, 242.

[26] Bergsma and Pitre, Kindle Location 19670.

Archaeologists seem to have also confirmed that the sacrificial, priestly worship that Amos refers to and corrects was, writes Bergsma and Pitre, "largely in line with the Mosaic regulations."[27] These Mosaic regulations are at times identified as part of the "Priestly" sections of the Pentateuch. Amos' knowledge of these Mosaic priestly laws, the archaeological evidence that worship was done in accordance with the "priestly" laws, and similarities between Amos and parts of the Pentateuch strongly indicate, contrary to Documentary Hypothesis assumption that "the prophets come before the law" as proposed by Wellhausen, that Amos and other prophetic portions of the Bible knew of the priestly parts of the Pentateuch and were at times inspired by it.[28] Amos' nine chapters, consequently, are composed   in

---

[27] Bergsma and Pitre, Kindle Location, 19685.

[28] Bergsma and Pitre, Kindle Location 19685. The following work is cited. Jonathan Samuel Greer, *Dinner at Dan: Biblical and Archaeological Evidence for Sacred Feasts at Iron Age II Tel Dan and Their Significance*, Culture and History of the Ancient Near East 66 (Leiden and Boston: Brill, 2013). ""Julius Wellhausen, who popularized the Documentary Hypothesis of the composition of the Pentateuch (JEDP), became convinced at a young age, probably for theological reasons, that 'the prophets preceded the law'; that is, the literary history of the religion of Israel is not truly as it appears to be in the Old Testament, in which Moses precedes the prophets. Rather, the literary prophets, starting with Amos, represent the 'original' religion of Israel, and later, when Israel was in an advanced state of cultural and religious decay after the exile, the bulk of the laws and liturgy of the Pentateuch (the 'Priestly source') were invented and retrojected into the mouth of Moses. One of the problems with this theory is that several prophets presuppose knowledge of the 'Priestly' portions of the Pentateuch. The most notable of these is Ezekiel, but the list includes Amos, who is often regarded as the oldest literary prophet."

continuity with and organically from the Pentateuch.[29]

Section Questions

1. Why, according to Miller, is the translation of Hebrew that Amos was a Shepherd not accurate? What is the more literal translation and what does tell the reader of Amos's social status? How is this indication of Amos's social status further confirmed by being a Dresser of Sycamore Trees?

2. In reference to Amos, how do Bergsma and Pitre argue that Wellhausen's view that the "prophets come before the law" unreasonable. Include the following in your response: archaeological evidence, Mosaic priestly laws.

Oracles (1:3-2:16)

The oracles are prophecies of divine chastisements against the Kingdom of Israel, the Kingdom of Judah, and nations that once were ruled by King David's and King Solomon's United Kingdom of Israel and Judah. Israel's transgressions include trampling "the head of the poor into the dust of earth" turning "aside the way of the afflicted," "a man and his father go[ing] into the same maiden," and false worship by laying "themselves down beside every altar (Amos 2:7-8 *RSVCE*)."[30] The last transgression of idolatry includes all the other transgressions since all the violations entail worshipping false gods whether in the form of idols or in the form of disordered pursuit of pleasure, power, and money. Worship of these false idols as the final end of life cause one to strive to have as much as possible of

---

[29] Compare Deuteronomy 28:38-40 with Amos 4:7-9. Bergsma and Pitre, Kindle Location 19680.

[30] Bergsma and Pitre, Kindle Location 19729.

the idol, with the ever-disappointed hope that a created, finite idol will satisfy the human heart, created only to be satisfied by the uncreated, infinite God. This false worship, in turn, leads to disregarding the needs of the poor, since the poor are not seen as brothers and sisters to take care of but, rather competitors for the limited resources of the idol that is worshipped.

The feverish striving to have as much pleasure, power and money led to the United Kingdom of Israel and Judah to be divided after the death of Solomon who had acquired 700 wives, 300 concubines (1 Kings 11:3), 666 talents of gold (1 Kings 10:14), and a vast amount of power. Solomon's addiction to money, power, pleasure and honor that people gave him, caused Solomon to want more and more without ever being satisfied by the salt-waters of death he was drinking since only God, the true water of life, satisfies our hearts created to love as God loves. God loves relationally as indicated in the Old Testament by his love relationship with Israel and by the revelation of the Trinity in the New Testament. Drinking the waters of eternal, divine life necessarily means abiding by God's relational, Trinitarian laws that move us away from selfish, excessively possessive love, to other centered love that gives away in joyful love that which we do not need, and others do need.[31]

---

[31] "Compendiums of the Social Doctrine of the Church," vatican.va, http://www.vatican.va/roman_curia/pontifical_councils/justpeace/docume nts/rc_pc_justpeace_doc_20060526_compendio-dott-soc_en.html#The%20relationship%20between%20principles%20and%20val ues, 34. "*The revelation in Christ of the mystery of God as Trinitarian love is at the same time the revelation of the vocation of the human person to love. This revelation sheds light on every aspect of the personal dignity and freedom of men and women, and on the depths of their social nature.* "Being a person in the image and likeness of God ... involves existing in a relationship, in relation to the other 'I'"[36], because God himself, one and triune, is the communion of the Father, of the Son and of the Holy Spirit."

Section Questions

1. How are all the sins condemned by Amos reducible to idolatry?

Judgments (3:1-5:6), Woes and Warnings (5:7-6:14)

In this section, Amos condemns the sins of Israel and warns of impending divine punishment. Amos begins with "Hear this word that the Lord has spoken against you, O sons of Israel, against the whole family which I brought up out of the land of Egypt: You only have I known of all the families of the earth (Amos 3:1-2 *RSVCE*)." As McConville observes, the Hebrew verb used for "known" can be translated in a variety of ways including "chosen" as it is in Genesis 18:19 when God says, in reference to Abraham, "I have chosen him (Genesis 18:19 RSVCE)."[32] The common root in both cases is *yada* (יָדַע).[33]

A reason for the punishments is that out of all the families on earth God chose Israel as the "firstborn son (Exodus 4:22 *RSVCE*)" to the nations. This privileged status bears with it honor and responsibilities, for Israel was chosen not for her own sake but for the sake of many, so that, gradually beginning with one people, all will be saved, "part by part (*CCC* 56)."[34]

The judgment facing Israel for having failed to live up to her chosen status is spread out over three chapters each of which begins with "Hear this word (Amos 3:1, 4:1, 5:1). These three "summons" to repentance, write Bergsma and Pitre, are followed by "the pronouncement of three 'woes' in the a new section of woes and warnings.[35]

---

[32] McConville, 167.

[33] "3045. yada," biblehub.com, https://biblehub.com/hebrew/3045.htm.

[34] "Catechism of the Catholic Church," no. 56, vatican.va, http://www.vatican.va/archive/ENG0015/__PG.HTM.

[35] Bergsma and Pitre, Kindle Location 19738.

Section Questions

1. As the firstborn son to the nations, how does Israel fail to live up to its obligations to "all the families of the earth (Amos 3:1-2)"? Include in your response the following: Chosen, Israel's role in Salvation History.

Visions (7:1-9:15)

In this section, Amos describes five visions he experienced: an invasion of destructive locusts, a consuming fire, God standing in judgment "with a plumb line in his hand (Amos 7:7 *RSVCE*)," a basket filled with summer harvest, and a vision of God "standing beside the altar (Amos 9:1 *RSVCE*) warning of impending punishment for Israel. The book ends, though, on a note of hope with God promising that "the days are coming ... when ... the mountains shall drip sweet wine, and all the hills shall flow with it. I will restore the fortunes of my people Israel .... I will plant them upon their land, and they shall never again be plucked up out of the land which I have given them (Amos 9:14-15 *RSVCE*)."

As Bergsma and Pitre observe, these verses call to mind the "peace and fertility" that Adam and Eve enjoyed before the Fall while in the Garden of Eden.[36] This Edenic, life-affirming peace, preaches Barron, is to radiate out from right worship as diversity is integrated, as diversity is "reconciled" with one another, as Pope Francis phrases it, in a peaceful manner according to the life-affirming message of the Good News of Jesus' Resurrection from the dead.[37] Our mission as disciples of Jesus is, asserts Barron, "to Edenize the

---

[36] Bergsma and Pitre, Kindle Location 19771.

[37] Robert Barron, *Priest, Prophet, King*, (Word on Fire Catholic Ministries, 2017), Lesson One, Adoratio; Francis, "Reconciled Diversity,"

whole world" to be "cultivators of a culture of life" that radiates out of our right worship.[38]

Amos's visions of the future contain a passage that seems to conflict with the central role of worship that Barron affirms as part of the restored Edenic order. The passage is in chapter seven which describes opposition that Amos received from the priest Amaziah. Amaziah commands Amos to "flee away to the land of Judah, and eat bread there, and prophecy there; but never again prophecy at Bethel, for it is the king's sanctuary, and it is the temple of the kingdom (Amos 7:12 *RSVCE*)."

Amaziah's strife with Amos has been interpreted as representing the inner-Biblical conflict between prophetic parts of the Old Testament with priestly parts. In this interpretation, Amos stands for the uncorrupted, original religious aspect of Israel, while Amaziah is represents the later corruption of Israelite religion in the form of a cultic, priestly centered religion. In opposing this reading Bergsma and Pitre write:

> The Old Testament does not recognize a distinction between "prophetic" and "priestly" religion. Some of the prophets were also priests or Levites: notably Ezekiel, Jeremiah, Zechariah, possibly Isaiah, and others. Ezekiel, Haggai, Zechariah, and Malachi were all very concerned about the proper function of the Temple, the priesthood, and the liturgy. The prophets do not critique public ritual worship *per se* but, rather, schismatic, syncretistic, hypocritical, and pagan forms of ritual.[39]

---

ewtn.com, https://www.ewtn.com/catholicism/library/reconciled-diversity-13103.

[38] Robert Barron, *Priest, Prophet, King*, (Word on Fire Catholic Ministries, 2017), Lesson One, Adoratio.

[39] Bergsma and Pitre, Kindle Location 19760.

Amos is concerned with purity of religion but not by abolishing the priesthood. Rather, he wants to purify the priesthood by insisting that unless one's life is morally acceptable to God, especially in how one's treats the poor and vulnerable of society, than no matter how many sacrifices and acts of worship are offered to God the priests and their sacrifices will rejected by God. As Miller explains, for Amos as with other prophets, "There is no cultic security blanket." In defining what he means by a "cultic security blanket," Miller assumes the role of a priest who believes that, Miller writes, "It's okay if I mistreat the poor because I performed the sacrifices God has asked for."

Miller phrases the same wrong assumption with, "God will pay no attention to my injustice so long as I continue the rituals of worship."[40] The hypocritical worship is the reason why Amos prophecies God telling Israel and its priests, "I hate, I despise your feasts, and I take no delight in your solemn assemblies. Even though you offer me your burnt offerings and cereal offerings, I will not accept them (Amos 5:21-22 RSVCE)." God rejects the acts of worship not because the acts of worship are intrinsically disordered but rather because the worship is offered by people who refuse to care for the poor, "because you trample upon the poor and take from him exactions of wheat (Amos 7:11 RSVCE)." For the "covenant relationship," as Miller phrases it, between God and Israel to be truly represented it is necessary for there to be a right relationship between Israel and the poor in their midst, otherwise righteousness, *tzedekah* (צְדָקָה), is lacking (Amos 5:7; 6:12).[41]

Section Questions

1. According to Bergsma and Pitre, is Amaziah's fight with Amos

---

[40] Miller, 243-244.

[41] "6666. tsedeqah," biblehub.com, https://www.biblehub.com/hebrew/6666.htm; Robert D. Miller II, *Understanding the Old Testament* (Chantilly: The Teaching Company, 2019), 243.

representative of a struggle between an earlier uncorrupted, prophetic form religion with a later corrupted, cultic, priestly centered religion? Include the following in your response: Priesthood, Public Ritual Worship, Temple Worship.

4. Obadiah

" And cast lots upon Jerusalem."—Obadiah i. 11.   42

Obadiah is only one chapter long and is the shortest book not only among the prophetic books but also in the entire Old Testament. The entire chapter is on Obadiah's vision in which God promises to humble the Kingdom of Edom. Edom borders the Kingdom of Judah's southern border. "You should not have rejoiced over the people of Judah in the day of their ruin" God tells Edom, "For the day of the Lord is near upon all the nations." God also promises that the "exiles of Jerusalem" shall return to "Mount Zion" to Jerusalem "and the kingdom shall be the Lord's."

As explained by Bergsma and Pitre, the clash between Edom and Israel was an ancient one. The origin of their strife is traced to the rivalry between twin brothers, Jacob and Esau, that was evident right from the moment of

---

42 "Vision of Obadiah," https://commons.wikimedia.org/wiki/ File:Obadiah.jpg.

their birth (Genesis 25:24-26).[43] Esau was born first. Jacob was born immediately after, with his hand holding his brother Esau's heel (Genesis 25:26). In Hebrew, Jacob's name (יַעֲקֹב) is based on the word meaning heel, since Jacob held his brother's heel.[44] A few verses later, Esau is given the name Edom for demanding the Jacob give him "red pottage, for I am famished! (Genesis 25:30 RSVCE)." Jacob refuses unless Esau gives him the privileges associated with being first-born, his "birth-right". Esau then "sold his birthright to Jacob. ... Thus, Esau despised his birthright (Genesis 25: 33-34 RSVCE)."

Esau's new name, Edom (אֱדֹם), meaning red in reference to the red food that he sold his birthright for.[45] In time Jacob also acquired a new name after he struggled with an angel and was named Israel, (יִשְׂרָאֵל), meaning God (el אֵל) and struggle/persevere (sarah שָׂרָה).[46] Throughout his life Jacob (Israel) struggled with his older brother Esau (Edom). The two brothers became the fathers of two nations, Israel and Edom, which continued this fraternal strife down the generations, including the time when Jesus was born. Shortly after Jesus was born, King Herod the Great, an Edomite, sought to kill Jesus along with all babies in Bethlehem "two years old or under (Matthew 2:16 RSVCE)."[47]

---

[43] Bergsma and Pitre, Kindle Location 19815.

[44] "3290. Yaaqob," biblehub.com, https://biblehub.com/hebrew/3290.htm.

[45] "123. edom," biblehub.com, https://biblehub.com/hebrew/123.htm.

[46] "8280. sarah," biblehub.com, https://biblehub.com/hebrew/8280.htm.

[47] Bergsma and Pitre, Kindle Location 19791; According to the ancient Jewish historian Flavius Josephus Herod "was no more than a private man, and an Idumean [a, i.e. a half Jew." Josephus, "Antiquities of the Jews, book 14, chapter 15, section 2," biblestudytools.com, https://www.biblestudytools.com/history/flavius-josephus/antiquities-jews-book-14/chapter-15.html. Josephus identifies Idumeans as Edomites. "these were

Jesus refers to family strife that includes the fraternal conflict between Jacob (Israel) and Esau (Edom) a conflict which directly affected Jesus as well: "Do not think that I have come to bring peace on earth; I have not come to bring peace, but a sword. I have come to set a man against his father, and a daughter against her mother, and a daughter-in-law against her mother-in-law; and a man's foes will be those of his own household (Matthew 10:34-36 *RSVCE*)." In the case of Herod the Great's strife with Jesus, a "sword" was directed against every baby boy two years old and younger with the intention to kill Jesus.

The example of Herod the Great teaches, that how and who one chooses to love is the source of family division. Those whose loves are properly other centered by being ordered to God, to Jesus, are in opposition to those, like Herod, who loves are centered on self, even if this means murdering others out of excessive self-love. St. Augustine in his *City of God* describes this conflict as two cities in opposition to one another: "Accordingly, two cities have been formed by two loves: the earthly by the love of self, even to the contempt of God; the heavenly by the love of God, even to the contempt of self."[48] Those whose loves are other centered "dwell," writes St. Augustine, "together in everlasting peace, in which self-love and self-will have no place,

---

the sons of Esau. Aliphaz had five legitimate sons; Theman, Omer, Saphus, Gotham, and Kanaz; for Amalek was not legitimate, but by a concubine, whose name was Thamna. These dwelt in that part of Idumea." Josephus, "Antiquities of the Jews, book 2, chapter 1, section 2," biblestudytools.com, https://www.biblestudytools.com/history/flavius-josephus/antiquities-jews/book-2/chapter-1.html. "So he fell upon the Idumeans, the posterity of Esau" Josephus, "Antiquities of the Jews, book 12, chapter 8, section 1," biblestudytools.com, https://www.biblestudytools.com/history/flavius-josephus/antiquities-jews/book-12/chapter-8.html.

[48] Augustine, *The City of God*, trans. J.F. Shaw (Veritatis Splendor Publications, 2012), book xiv, chapter 28, 359.

but a ministering love that rejoices in the common joy of all, of many hearts makes one, that is to say, secures a perfect accord."[49]

Love of Jesus necessarily entails properly other centered love and rejection of love that is or tends to be exclusively self-centered for as Pope Francis teaches, quoting Jesus, "God's word teaches that our brothers and sisters are the prolongation of the incarnation for each of us: 'As you did it to one of these, the least of my brethren, you did it to me' (Mt 25:40)."[50] Obadiah teaches us about the social nature of salvation, that salvation entails being a member of certain community, a city, a city of those whose loves are ordered to love of God, and through God, to one's brothers and sisters, for Jesus came to redeem, teaches Pope Francis quoting from the *Compendium of the Social Doctrine of the Church*, "not only the individual person, but also the social relations existing between men."[51]

Section Questions

1. How is the Kingdom of Edom related to a sibling rivalry and who were these two children?

---

[49] Augustine, *The City of God*, trans. J.F. Shaw (Veritatis Splendor Publications, 2012), book xiv, chapter 1, 359.

[50] Francis, *The Complete Encyclicals, Bulls, and Apostolic Exhortations, Volume I* (Notre Dame: Ave Maria Press, 2016), 138. The quotation is from *Evangelii Gaudium* no. 179.

[51] Francis, 137. The quotation is from *Compendium of the Social Doctrine of the Church* no. 52.

5. Jonah

Introduction

The very first verse identifies Jonah as "the son of Amittai (Jonah 1:1 *RSVCE*)." The text provides few other details about Jonah that would help to identify him historically. The second book of Kings, though, refers to a prophet named Jonah who may be the Jonah of the book of Jonah especially since not only is Jonah mentioned but he is also named "the son of Amittai (2 Kings 14:25 *RSVCE*)." This Jonah prophesied during the reign of the King of Israel, Jeroboam II (c. 780s-740s B.C.) Presuming the Jonah in the second book of Kings is the same as the Jonah in the book of Jonah, then Jonah prophesied shortly before the Assyrians in 722 B.C. conquered the Northern Kingdom of Israel and deported her people.

[52] Metropolitan Museum of Art / Public domain, "Jonah and the giant fish in the Jami' al-tawarikh (c. 1400), Metropolitan Museum of Art,"

Due to the difficulty in dating Jonah, to the lack non-biblical records referring to the Ninevites repenting, and certain miraculous aspects of the book, including Jonah's survival after being swallowed by a huge fish, many modern biblical scholars deem the book of Jonah as fiction.[53] Bergsma and Pitre, though, counter this modern view with "ancient Jewish and Christian tradition is unanimous in regarding the book as a historical narrative of miraculous events (cf. Tob 14:4; 3 Mac 6:8). A notable example of this may be the saying of Jesus in the Gospel of Matthew, in which he prophesies the historical event of his Resurrection by reference to a previous event."[54] As the four chapters are outlined, these comments of Bergsma and Pitre on the miraculous survival of Jonah will be discussed.

Section Questions

1. Contrast the traditional view of the historicity of Jonah with the dominant modern view. Include the following in your response: Miracles, Ninevites.

Chapter One: Jonah Disobeys God

In chapter one, Jonah refuses to obey God who commands Jonah to travel to the Assyrian city of Nineveh in the south to preach a message of repentance. Knowing that the Assyrians were great persecutors of his people, Jonah refuses and flees on a ship going to Tarshish. God responds by sending

---

https://commons.wikimedia.org/wiki/File:Jonah_and_the_Whale,_Folio_from_a_Jami_al-Tavarikh_(Compendium_of_Chronicles).jpg.

[53] Irene Nowell, *New Collegeville Bible Commentary: Old Testament* (Collegeville: Liturgical Press, 2015), Kindle Location 90.

[54] John Bergsma and Brant Pitre, *A Catholic Introduction to the Bible, Volume I* (San Francisco: Ignatius Press, 2018), Kindle Location 19842.

a storm that threatens to capsize the ship. Upon casting lots, the crew suspect Jonah as the reason for the storm. Jonah admits this is true, confesses he is fleeing from God's will, and tells the crew to "throw me into the sea (Jonah 1:12 *RSVCE*)." Eventually, the men throw Jonah, the sea calms, Jonah is swallowed by a giant fish, "and Jonah was in the belly of the fish three days and three nights (1 Jonah 1:17 *RSVCE*)."

Captive in the belly of the fish, Jonah was given time to be purified of his false understanding of God and, consequently, of his idolatry, for although Jonah thought he was worshipping the true God he was doing so only in part, for God in His true fullness is not a God only of the nation of Israel but is a God of all people as Jesus will later teach with God "makes his sun rise on the evil and on the good, and sends rain on the just and the unjust. ... And if you salute only your brethren, what more are you doing than others? Do not even the Gentiles do the same? You, therefore, must be perfect, as your heavenly Father is perfect (Matthew 5:45-48 *RSVCE*)." In accordance with the teaching of Jonah, Jesus commands love of not only one's neighbor but also of one's enemy, in the case of Jonah of the Assyrians who were enemies of Israel: "You have heard that it was said, 'You shall love your neighbor and hate your enemy.' But I say to you, love your enemies and pray for those who persecute you, so that you may be sons of your Father who is in heaven (Matthew 5:43-45 *RSVCE*)."

Section Questions

1. How does Jonah mission to the Ninevites anticipate the New Testament, specifically Jesus' teaching to love enemies?

Chapter Two and Three: Both Jonah and the Ninevites Repent

After being spewed out by the fish, Jonah, in chapter three, reluctantly obeys God and goes to Nineveh to preach a message of repentance and of divine mercy for those who repent. By so doing Jonah, however imperfectly, was fulfilling Israel's election of being called for the sake of the many. As God says, "Israel is my firstborn son (Exodus 4:22 *RSVCE*)." Israel is the first among nations as firstborn son not to bask in glory in its special election but to recognize her responsibility to her younger brothers and sisters which entails leading all nations to worship the true God. One day, Isaiah prophecies, following Israel's lead, people of all nations will worship God in the Holy City of Jerusalem (Isaiah 2:1-4).

Jonah's three days and three nights in the belly of a fish is quoted by Jesus: "For as Jonah was three days and three nights in the belly of the whale, so will the Son of Man be three days an three nights in the heart of the earth (Matthew 12:40 *RSVCE*)." The divine Son of Man, Jesus, fulfills this prophecy by rising from the dead. When the prayer of Jonah in chapter two is closely looked at, the connection between Jonah and Judah becomes more apparent. As Bergsma and Pitre observe, the text describes Jonah as not just crying out to God from the belly of the fish but as crying out from Sheol (שְׁאוֹל), the place where people go after dying (Jonah 2:2).

The two scholars comment, "Perhaps we are to understand the prophet as dying in the fish, later to be expelled and resurrected. If so, then Jesus' comparison of his own death and Resurrection to the 'sign of Jonah' becomes completely explicable (cv. Mt 12:38-41)."[55] Thus understood, explain Bergsma and Pitre, Jonah's miraculous survival was due not to having been kept alive in the belly of a fish but rather having died in the fish, descended to the real of the dead and then raised from the dead by God who wanted Jonah to complete his mission of preaching divine mercy to Ninevites.[56]

Upon reaching Nineveh, Jonah cries out throughout the city, "Yet forty days, and Nineveh shall be overthrown! (Jonah 3:4 *RSVCE*)" Hearing this call to repentance, the Ninevites repent "from the greatest of them to the least of

---

[55] Bergsma and Pitre, Kindle Location 19886.

[56] Bergsma and Pitre, Kindle Location 19886.

them (Jonah 3:5 *RSVCE*)" including the king. God responds by not allowing Nineveh to be overthrown.

Section Questions

1. How does Jonah being swallowed by a fish foreshadow the New Testament? Include the following in your response: Sheol.
2. How is Jonah's preaching to the Ninevites in accordance with Israel's election as first born of the nations (Exodus 4:22)?

Chapter Four: Jonah Argues with God

Instead of rejoicing that the Ninevites had repented and God had withheld punishment, Jonah becomes angry with God for being merciful to the Ninevites. In his resentful rage, Jonah even tells God to "take my life away from me (Jonah 4:3 *RSVCE*)." Jonah angerly leaves the city and sits down, sulking. God causes a plant to miraculously grow, providing Jonah shade from the beating sun. When dawn comes, a worm gnaws on the plant; the plant withers; God sends a wind, and the sun beats down upon Jonah's unprotected head. Once again Jonah complains, "It is better for me to die than to live (Jonah 4:8 *RSVCE*)." God reprimands Jonah by telling him that if Jonah can so easily feel pity for a plant than all the more should God have pity on the Ninevites.

Jonah's resentment, and self-pity which leads him down the road of despair where he even toys with the temptation to allow himself to die is a common diabolical temptation that addicts face, and ultimately all sinners face since sinning is a type of addiction. As Fr. Groeschel states:

When we are discouraged and wallow in discouragement and depression, we set ourselves up to fall into temptation. This is frequently acknowledged by people in AA meetings. The devil is the father of lies. He wants to convince people that they have no hope which leads to despair. ... A struggling saint who manages to smile is following Mother Teresa and other saints like her.[57]

Jonah's resentful self-pity was due to his anger that God looked upon the Ninevites favorably. In contrast, Jesus teaches, "there will be more joy in heaven over one sinner who repents than over nine-nine righteous persons who need no repentance (Luke 15:7 *RSVCE*)." Applying Jesus' teaching to our times, Pope Francis writes:

> Whenever our interior life becomes caught up in its own interests and concerns, there is no longer room for others, no place for the poor. God's voice is no longer heard, the quiet joy of his love is no longer felt, and the desire to do good fades. This is a very real danger for believers too. Many fall prey to it, and end up resentful, angry and listless. That is no way to live a dignified and fulfilled life; it is not God's will for us, nor is it the life in the Spirit which has its source in the heart of the risen Christ.[58]

The book of Jonah points us in the direction of Jesus who wishes us to be His preachers, who evangelize the world not resentfully, or angerly but with joy, and hope that as many people as possible will embrace the Good News of God's divine mercy and then rejoice when people repent and grow in holiness, including when the holiness of those who repent, the intimacy with God of those who repent, surpasses the holiness and intimacy with God

---

[57] Benedict Groeschel, Sunday Night Live recording, October 14, 2007, EWTN.

[58] Francis, "*Apostolic Exhortation Evangelii Gaudium*, 2013," vatican.va, http://www.vatican.va/content/francesco/en/apost_exhortations/document s/papa-francesco_esortazione-ap_20131124_evangelii-gaudium.html, no. 2.

of those who preached the Good News to them. In contrast with Jonah, may we pray as Cardinal Merry del Val humbly and joyfully prayed without envy or resentment, "That others may be more holy than I, provided I may become as holy as I should. Jesus, grant me the grace to desire it."[59]

Section Questions

1. When the plant that Jonah is under and which is providing shade from the sun for Jonah dies, how does God respond to Jonah's complaints?

6. Micah

Like Jonah's preaching which was well received by the Ninevites who repented, Micah's preaching was well received by the people of Judah who repented of their errant ways. In both cases, God responded by saving the repentant from harm. The Second Book of Kings and Isaiah describes this salvific time under the reign of King Hezekiah who, upon listening to the prophet Isaiah, repented along with the people of Judah (2 Kings 19; Isaiah 37). The first verse of Micah locates Micah as living in the times of the Judean kings, "Jotham, Ahaz, and Hezekiah (Micah 1:1 *RSVCE*)." This means that at the same time Isaiah was preaching a message of repentance to the Judeans, Micah was also preaching. As Bergsma and Pitre observe, the prophet Jeremiah explicitly identifies Micah as prophesying to King Hezekiah: "Micah of Moresheth prophesied in the days of Hezekiah king of Judah (Jeremiah 26:18 *RSVCE*)."[60]

---

[59] An excerpt from Rafael Cardinal Merry del Val's *Litany of Humility*.

[60] John Bergsma and Brant Pitre, *A Catholic Introduction to the Bible, Volume I* (San Francisco: Ignatius Press, 2018), Kindle Location 19943.

Introduction

The prophet Micah's name is a reference to God's mercy to the repentant, in particular to the repentant Judean. Micah is an abbreviation of Micayah (מִיכָיָה), meaning who is like (*Mi ca* מִיכָ) God (YH יָה).[62] Chapter seven answers why no one is like God with, "Who is a God like you, pardoning iniquity and passing over transgression ... He does not retain his anger forever because he delights in mercy (Micah 7:18 *RSVCE*)."

McConville outlines the basic structure of Micah around condemnation and mercy in three parts: Sin Denounced and a Remnant Gathered (chapters 1-2), Condemnation and Redemption (chapters 3-5), Lament and

---

[61] Gustave Doré / Public domain, "Engraving of the Prophet Micah by Gustave Doré," https://commons.wikimedia.org/wiki/File:139.Micah_Exhorts_the_Israelites_to_Repent.jpg.

[62] "4318. Mikah," biblehub.com, https://biblehub.com/hebrew/4318.htm.

Forgiveness (chapter 6-7).[63]

Section Questions

1. What does Micah's name mean in Hebrew?

Remnant Gathered Chapters 1-2

The first verse locates Micah as prophesying in the reigns of three southern kings: Jotham (ca. 742-735 B.C.) Ahaz (ca. 735-715 B.C.), and King Hezekiah (ca. 715-687 B.C.). Under King Ahaz's reign over the Southern Kingdom of Judah, the Assyrian Empire invaded the Northern Kingdom of Israel. In 722 B.C., the Assyrians sacked the Northern Kingdom of Samaria in 722 B.C. and deported many of the people of Israel (2 Kings 17:1-6). King Ahaz's son, Hezekiah, inherited the throne and ruled over Judah. Heeding Isaiah's and Micah's prophecies, King Hezekiah instituted renewed worship of the true God by abolishing idolatry and hypocritical practices throughout his kingdom.

As Hahn describes the course of events, Hezekiah abided his time patiently under Assyrian rule.[64] He chose to rebel against Assyrian oppression, when the Assyrian Empire was fragile during a time of political transition from King Sargon's rule to his successor King Sennacherib in 705 B.C. Sennacherib responded by mobilizing his troops to attack Judah, but:

that night the angel of the Lord went forth and slew a hundred and

---

[63] Gordon J. McConville, *Exploring the Old Testament: A Guide to the Prophets: 4 Exploring the Bible Series* (Downers Grove: InterVarsity Press, 2002), 197.

[64] Scott Hahn, *Catholic Bible Dictionary* (New York: Doubleday, 2009), 360.

eighty-five thousand in the camp of the Assyrians; and when men arose early in the morning, behold, these were all dead bodies. Then Sennacherib king of Assyria departed, and went home, and dwelt at Nineveh. And as he was worshiping in the house of Nisroch his god, Adrammelech and Sharezer, his sons, slew him with the sword, and escaped into the land of Ararat. And Esarhaddon his son reigned in this stead (2 Kings 19:35-37 *RSVCE*).

During these times of invasion Micah warns of impending destruction of the Northern capital city of Samaria, and the destruction of the Southern capital city of Jerusalem, representing the people of the Southern King of Judah (Micah 1).

Shifting away from the sins of the people to the mercy of God, in chapter two God promises that He will "gather the remnant of Israel; I will set them together like sheep in a fold (Micah 2:12 *RSVCE*)."

Section Questions

1. How, according to Micah, will God relate in the end to the "remnant of Israel (Micah 2:12)."

Condemnation and Redemption Chapters 3-5

Chapters three through five repeat the pattern of God denouncing evil and then promising a time of redemption. In chapter three, God denounces rulers to oppress their people, and false prophets who lead people astray. Because of this wickedness, "Jerusalem shall become a heap of ruins (Micah 3:12 *RSVCE*)." This denouncement of sin is followed by chapter four where God promises to restore Jerusalem where it will one day become a city on Mount Zion where "many nations shall come (Micah 4:2 *RSVCE*)" to be taught the ways of God. Then, in chapter five a saving ruler from Judah, from the birthplace of King David, Bethlehem, is promised:

> But you, O Bethlehem Ephrathah, who are little to be among the clans of Judah, from you shall come forth for me one who is to be rule in Israel, whose origin is from of old, from ancient days. Therefore, he shall give them up until the time when she who has labor pains has brought forth; then the rest of his brethren shall return to the sons of Israel (Micah 5:2-3 *RSVCE*).

Traditionally, this prophecy has been interpreted as fulfilled in the birth of Jesus Christ head and members. First, Jesus was born of Mary, born of a Virgin, in the town of Bethlehem. His "origin is from of old, from ancient days" since Jesus is the Son of God. Second, Mary gave birth also to the members of Jesus' Mystical Body the Church who were born outside of Jerusalem on Golgotha in Bethlehem. Unlike when giving birth to the head of the Mystical Body, Jesus, Mary experienced spiritual "labor pains" while standing at the foot of the Cross as she gave birth to the body, which is the Church as Christ's presence sacramentally extended through time. As Hans Urs von Balthasar comments, "In the birth pangs of the Cross, the Woman, Mary, gives birth to the brothers and sisters of the Messiah."[65]

Section Questions

1. When and how does Mary contribute to the fulfillment of the following prophecy? Include in your response the following:

---

[65] Hans Urs Von Balthasar, "Mary Archetype of the Church According to Hans Von Balthasar," christendom-awake.org, http://christendom-awake.org/pages/mcbride/mary-vonb.htm, chapter 2, C; Alberto Ferreiro, *Ancient Christian Commentary on Scripture, Old Testament XIV, The Twelve Prophets* (Downers Grove: InterVarsity Press, 2003), 297-302.

Bethlehem, labor pains. "But you, O Bethlehem Ephrathah, who are little to be among the clans of Judah, from you shall come forth for me one who is to be rule in Israel, whose origin is from of old, from ancient days. Therefore, he shall give them up until the time when she who has labor pains has brought forth; then the rest of his brethren shall return to the sons of Israel (Micah 5:2-3 *RSVCE*)."

Lament and Forgiveness Chapter 6-7

The concluding chapters once again repeat the pattern of condemnation followed by mercy. Chapter six condemns those who worship God with the assumption that the worship will excuse their sins, when precisely the opposite takes place since "thousands of rams" who are sacrificed to God will not justify sins. What God wants is his adopted children "to do justice, and to love kindness, and to walk humbly with your God (Micah 6:8 *RSVCE*)."

Expressing this desire, Jesus teaches, "if you are offering your gift at the altar, and there remember that your brother has something against you, leave your gift there before the altar and go; first be reconciled to your brother, and then come and offer your gift (Matthew 5:24 *RSVCE*)." In other words, the sacrifices at the altar ought to be done "without neglecting the others (Matthew 11:42 *RSVCE*), without neglecting justice and charity to our brothers and sisters otherwise our sacrifices, our worship is in vain.

This condemnation of hypocritical worship is followed by a denouncement of rich who use their wealth not as an opportunity to be generous to the needy but as a means to oppress to "be full of violence (Micah 6:12 *RSVCE*)" and of rulers who use their power "to ask for a bribe (Micah 7:3 *RSVCE*)."

Chapter seven concludes the book of Micah with trust in God's infinite mercy and faithfulness to his covenant of love with his people: "Who is a God like you, pardoning iniquity and passing over transgression for the remnant of his inheritance? He does not retain his anger forever because he delights in mercy. ... You will show faithfulness to Jacob and mercy to Abraham, as you have sworn to our fathers from the days of old (Micah 7:18-20 *RSVCE*)."

Section Questions

1. Does Micah conclude on message of mercy or on a concluding note of impending punishment? What does Micah's conclusion reveal about God's nature?

7. Nahum

Like Jonah, Nahum also directly involves the Assyrian capital city of Nineveh. Unlike Jonah, Nahum does not prophecy the salvation of Nineveh but its destruction. Nahum prophesied Nineveh's destruction sometime between, state Bergsma and Pitre, "663 B.C. and 612 B.C." the dates of the destruction of the Egyptian city Thebes, which Nahum refers to in chapter

---

[66] James Tissot / Public domain, "Nahum (watercolor circa 1888 by James Tissot)," https://commons.wikimedia.org/wiki/File:Nahum.jpg.

three (8-10), and the destruction of Nineveh by the Babylonians and Medes, which Nahum predicts will take place.[67]

Verse one identifies Nahum's hometown as Elkosh, whose location is unknown. It is also not clear from the text if Nahum is from the southern or northern kingdom. Although, it is evident, as chapter three indicates, that Nahum preached before the northern Kingdom of Israel fell in 722 B.C., when both the northern and southern kingdom were intact.

The introductory verse is followed by Nahum praising God who is "avenging and wrathful (Nahum 1:2 *RSVCE*)" who although "slow to anger ... will be no means clear the guilty (Nahum 1:3 RSVCE)" because "The Lord is good (Nahum 1:7 *RSVCE*)." Chapter two then focuses on the evil behavior in Nineveh which God in his goodness will not tolerate: "Nineveh is like a pool whose waters run away. ... Desolation and ruin (Nahum 2:8, 10 *RSVCE*)." Chapter three then concludes Nahum by speaking of the destruction of Nineveh: "Woe to the bloody city, all full of lies and booty – no end to the plunder. ... Wasted is Nineveh; who will moan over her? (Nahum 3:1, 7 *RSVCE*)."

Nahum's prophecy of the Assyrian Empire's fall, and that its capital city Nineveh will be "wasted" likely was viewed by many who heard Nahum as hard to believe since the Assyrian Empire appeared invincible. As McConville writes, "If you had been a Judean, or indeed a Syrian or an Egyptian, when Assyria was overrunning its neighbors, it might have seemed as if its power would never come to an end."[68] The prophecy, though, came true when in c. 612 B.C. the powerful city of Nineveh fell to the armies of the Babylonians and Medes. The Babylonians then became the dominant world

---

[67] John Bergsma and Brant Pitre, *A Catholic Introduction to the Bible, Volume I* (San Francisco: Ignatius Press, 2018), Kindle Location 20070.

[68] Gordon J. McConville, *Exploring the Old Testament: A Guide to the Prophets: 4 Exploring the Bible Series* (Downers Grove: InterVarsity Press, 2002), 208.

power and the Ninevites power vanished as a cloud of destroying locusts disappear at the break of day: "[T]hey fly away; no one knows where they are (Nahum 3:17 *RSVCE*)."

Nineveh's destruction contrast with the Ninevites earlier experiencing God's mercy upon hearing Jonah's preaching and repenting. The two books of Jonah and Nahum with two distinctly different outcomes form the reality of justice and mercy which mutually inform one another. One without the other does not truly exist, nor does one contradict the other for, as Pope Francis writes, they are "two dimensions of a single reality," God "the fullness of love."[69] Jonah emphasizes the merciful dimension of God, while Nahum brings out the just dimension of God. "Jonah," writes Bergsma and Pitre, "reminds us that God's mercy and forgiveness are available even to hardened sinners. Nahum reminds us that the window of opportunity to avail ourselves of this mercy can indeed come to a close, both for individuals and for nations."[70]

Similar to Nahum, Benedict XVI cautions us not to "forget … that the God of reason and of love is also the Judge of the world and of mankind—the guarantor of justice, to whom men must render an accounting. Given the temptations to power, it is a fundamental obligation to keep in mind the truth about the Judgment: every one of us must someday give an account. There is a justice that is not abolished by love."[71] Love for the weak and defenseless at times requires resistance to abusive power Benedict XVI asserts: "An absolute pacifism that refused to grant the law any effective means for its enforcement would be a capitulation to injustice. It would

---

[69] Francis, "*Misericordiae Vultus*, Bull of Indiction of the Extraordinary Jubilee of Mercy, 2015," no. 20.

[70] Bergsma and Pitre, Kindle Location 20129.

[71] Joseph Ratzinger, *Europe, Today and Tomorrow: Addressing the Fundamental Issues*, trans. J. Miller (San Francisco: Ignatius Press, 2007), 97-98.

sanction the seizure of power by this injustice and would surrender the world to the dictatorship of force."[72]

Section Questions

1. With respect to Nineveh and repentance, contrast with Jonah with Nahum and explain how these two books complement one another.

8. Habakkuk

In the chapter on Nahum, Nahum was compared and contrasted with Jonah. Habakkuk also can be compared and contrasted with Jonah. Unlike the other minor prophets, Habakkuk and Jonah are not primarily prophecies directed towards Israel or other nations but rather are essentially an argument that Habakkuk and Jonah have with God. "Both Jonah and Habakkuk" explains Bergsma and Pitre "struggle with the justice of God's ways. The book of Jonah explores this question largely through narrative, whereas Habakkuk addresses it through dialogue between the prophet and the Lord."[73]

Another difference between Jonah and Habakkuk is the historical context. Jonah prophesied during the time of Assyrian dominance. Habakkuk prophesied when the Babylonians replaced the Assyrians as the dominant power. Verse six of chapter one provides this historical context: "I [God] am rousing the Chaldeans [Babylonians]...to seize habitations not their own (Habakkuk 1:6 *RSVCE*)." McConville interprets this verse as a

---

[72] Joseph Ratzinger, *Values in a Time of Upheaval: Meeting the Challenges of the Future*, trans. Brian McNeil (San Francisco: Ignatius Press, 2006), Kindle location, 1282.

[73] Bergsma and Pitre, Kindle Location 20129.

reference to the Babylonian conquest of the Ninevites in 612 B.C.[74]

Habakkuk's struggle with God permitting the Babylonians to oppress the Jewish people is in three chapters. In first chapter Habakkuk questions God's justice: "You who are of purer eyes than to behold evil and cannot look on wrong, why do you look on faithless men, and are silent when the wicked swallows up the man more righteous than he (Habakkuk 1:13 *RSVCE*)."

The second chapter presents God's answer to Habakkuk's bewilderment in the face of evil. The book concludes with Habakkuk accepting God's response as a mystery that cannot be clearly understood: "Though the fig tree does not blossom, nor fruit be on the vines, the produce of the olive fail and the fields yield no food, the flock be cut off from the fold and there be no herds in the stalls, yet I will rejoice in the Lord, I will joy in the God of my salvation (Habakkuk 3:17-18 *RSVCE*)."

Habakkuk intersperses questions in his cry of complaint to God in chapter one. He asks how much time it will take for God to answer him (verse

---

[74] McConville, 211.

[75] Ariel Palmon / CC BY (https://creativecommons.org/licenses/by/3.0, "Tomb of Habakkuk near Kadarim, Israel," https://commons. wikimedia.org/wiki/File:Prophet_Habakkuk_Tomb_ap_002.jpg.

2). He points out that since God is all "Holy One" why does God remain silent in the face of evil (verses 12-13). In these same verses, Habakkuk also questions the justice of punishing the Jewish people through the Chaldeans (Babylonians) who have done far greater evil than the Jewish people have (verse 13). God responds be encouraging patient waiting: "If it seems slow, wait for it; it will surely come, it will not delay (Habakkuk 2:3 *RSVCE*)." God waits since God respects the process that Judea needs to undergo to be healed of her sins in such a way that she will more likely in freedom return to God and to holy ways of living. God did not directly punish the Jewish people through the Babylonians rather God allowed sin to take its natural course of punishing those who sin with the intention that in the process the Jewish people will mature in their relationship with God. As Joan Chittister well phrases how we are punished: "God does not punish sin,' Julian [of Norwich] teaches. 'Sin punishes sin.'"[76]

This teaching on patiently trusting that God is rendering justice through healing processes that at times are painful to endure is similar, observes McConville, to the Letter to the Hebrews which states, "For you have need of endurance, so that you may do the will of God and receive what is promised. 'For yet a little while, and the coming one shall come and shall not tarry; but my righteous one shall live by faith, and if he shrinks back, my soul has no pleasure in him.' But we are not of those who shrink back and are destroyed, but of those who have faith and keep their souls (Hebrews 10:36-39 *RSVCE*)."[77]

Verse thirty-seven from chapter ten of Hebrews is an echo of verse four, chapter two of Habakkuk: "[T]he righteous shall live by his faith (Habakkuk 2:4 *RSVCE*)." The Hebrew word that is translated by faith is *Emunah* (אֱמוּנָה) which comes from the root word *aman* (אָמַן). Words indicating a reality that

---

[76] Joan Chittister, *For Everything A Season* (New York: Orbis Books, 2013), 73.

[77] McConville, 217.

endures, and hence supports and confirms are based on the root *aman*, including the noun truth, *emeth* (אֱמֶת).[78] The English word Amen is also derived from the root *aman* and when used indicates agreement in the truth of something or some person. The prime examples in the Old Testament of righteous ones who lived by faith, who consistently gave their Amen to God by trusting God's promises are true, are Abel, Enoch, Noah, Abraham, and Moses, all whom are cited in Hebrews (chapter 11).

The cited passages indicate that faith and truth are biblically interrelated to one another since they share in a reality that endures and lasts. The most truthful reality is God since God simply is, without beginning or end. God's love is most true since God's love is without beginning or end and therefore endures, supports and confirms eternally. Only by participating in the uncreated truth of God can human beings relate to one another for, writes Benedict XVI, "truth…is the medium in which men make contact, whereas it is the absence of truth which closes them off from one another." [79]

Chapter three consists of a prayer by which the prophet affirms his trust in God and commits himself to "quietly wait (Habakkuk 3:16 *RSVCE*)" confident that one day "I will rejoice in the Lord (Habakkuk 3:18 *RSVCE*)." This joy is not something that is relegated to the future but is also experienced by Habakkuk as a reality that is here but not fully yet since the reality the prophet is referring to is God who is with Habakkuk and whom Habakkuk is called to one day be fully united with. Habakkuk's faithful trust that God will one day save his people and crush "the head of the wicked (Habakkuk 3:13 *RSVCE*)" is answered in an unexpected way by the crucifixion of Jesus on the cross which is the ultimate "sign" of God's faithful

---

[78]   "530. emunah, 571. emeth, 539. aman," biblehub.com, https://biblehub.com/hebrew/539.htm.

[79] Joseph Ratzinger, *The Nature and Mission of Theology: Essays to Orient Theology in Today's Debates*, trans. A. Walker (San Francisco: Ignatius Press, 1995), 38-39.

true love. Often, though, like Habakkuk we want God to be different, as Benedict XVI describes:

> How often we wish that God would make show himself stronger, that he would strike decisively, defeating evil and creating a better world. All ideologies of power justify themselves in exactly this way, they justify the destruction of whatever would stand in the way of progress and the liberation of humanity. We suffer on account of God's patience. And yet, we need his patience. God, who became a lamb, tells us that the world is saved by the Crucified One, not by those who crucified him. The world is redeemed by the patience of God. It is destroyed by the impatience of man.[80]

Section Questions

1. With respect literary form, how specifically are Jonah and Habakkuk similar and different?
2. How is the word Amen related to faith and truth and how does faith relate to patient, trusting waiting in Habakkuk?

9. Zephaniah

The book opens by introducing Zephaniah as receiving "the word of the Lord" during the days of King Josiah (c. 640-609 B.C.) who ruled over the

---

[80] Benedict XVI, "Mass, Imposition of the Pallium and Conferral of the Fisherman's Ring for the Beginning of the Petrine Ministry of the Bishop of Rome: Homily of His Holiness Benedict XVI, St. Peter's Square, Sunday, 24 April 2005," w2.vatican.va, https://w2.vatican.va/content/benedict-xvi/en/homilies/2005/documents/hf_ben-xvi_hom_20050424_inizio-pontificato.html.

southern Kingdom of Judea. During his rule, Josiah headed a reform movement by first purifying the Jerusalem Temple and other places of worship from idolatrous practices (2 Chronicles 34:3-7). In the midst of purging Judea from idolatry, "the book of the law" was found and read to Josiah. Upon hearing "the words of the book of the law (2 Kings 22:11 *RSVCE*)" Josiah felt profoundly convicted of sin and committed himself to reforming his kingdom even further by reading the book of the law to "all the people, both small and great (2 Kings 23:2 *RSVCE*)."

Afterwards, the king publicly renewed the Judean people's covenant with

[81] Unknown author / Public domain, "Josiah hearing the book of the law (1873)," https://commons.wikimedia.org/wiki/File:Josiah_hearing_the_book_of_the_law.jpg.

God. This was then followed by further removal of idolatrous practices from both the Northern Kingdom of Israel and from the Southern Kingdom of Judah. Finally, Josiah commanded his people to "Keep the Passover to the Lord your God, as it is written in this book of the covenant (2 Kings 21)." After many generations of not celebrating the Passover, the Jewish people once again celebrated the Passover.

In a way not explicitly stated, Zephaniah helped to inspire, support and sustain King Josiah's reform. Zephaniah's prophetic call to reform is in three main parts. In chapter one Zephaniah preaches on "the Day of the Lord" when all will be judged by God (1:1-18). This is followed by divine judgments on specific nations in the second chapter and part of the third chapter (2-3:8). The book ends with a hope filled prophecy of Israel's restoration (3:9-20 *RSVCE*).

As other prophets had, Zephaniah uses the terminology "Day of the Lord" in the context of a call to reform. Zephaniah does so by describing the

---

[82] John Martin / Public domain, "The End of the World, also known as The Great Day of His Wrath by John Martin," https://commons.wikimedia.org/wiki/File:John_Martin_-_The_Great_Day_of_His_Wrath_-_Google_Art_Project.jpg.

Day of the Lord as a liturgical event when God will purify the world by ending false worship "on the day of the wrath of the Lord (Zephaniah 1:18 *RSVCE*)." True worship "on the day of the LORD'S sacrifice (Zephaniah 1:8 *RSVCE*)" will then take place. Chapter two's condemnations of specific nations also refers to "the day of the wrath of the LORD (Zephaniah 2:3 *RSVCE*)." Not only will idolaters be punished on the day of wrath but also those who have roles that hold them to a higher standard of morality specifically, judges, prophets, priests, and "officials" who "are roaring lions ... evening wolves (Zephaniah 3:3 *RSVCE*)."

Instead of living out their roles of leadership by service these "officials," comment McConville, instead use their positions of power for self-gain by abusing those under their power.[83] In response, God will "pour out ... all the heat of my anger (Zephaniah 3:8 *RSVCE*)." However, God will allow a "remnant (Zephaniah 2:9 *RSVCE*)" to survive and will transform "the speech of the peoples to a pure speech, that all of them may call on the name of the LORD (Zephaniah 3:9 *RSVCE*)." Purified of pride, this people will be "humble and lowly ... they shall do no wrong and utter no lies, nor shall there be found in their mouth a deceitful tongue (Zephaniah 3:12-13 *RSVCE*)."

Saint Fulgentius of Ruspe (c. 462-533) interpreted the "the pure speech" as fulfilled in the celebration of the Sacraments of the New Testament, above all by the Sacrament of the Mass. According to Fulgentius, Zephaniah prophesied the "New Testament" when:

> spiritual sacrifices were to be offered not to the Father only but also to the Son by the faithful. For Zephaniah says, "'Therefore wait for me,' says the Lord, 'for the day when I arise as a witness. For my decision is to gather nations, to assemble kingdoms, to pour out on

---

[83] Gordon J. McConville, *Exploring the Old Testament: A Guide to the Prophets: 4 Exploring the Bible Series* (Downers Grove: InterVarsity Press, 2002), 226.

them my indignation, all the heat of my anger; for in the fire of my passion, all the earth shall be consumed. At the time I will change the speech of the peoples to a pure speech, that all of them may call on the name of the Lord and serve him with one accord. From beyond the rivers of Ethiopia, my suppliants, my scattered ones, shall bring my offering."[84]

Resonating with Fulgentius's commentary, John Chrysostom similarly interprets verse eleven of chapter two prophecy that on the Day of the Lord people from all nations will "bow down" in worship of God "each in its place, all the lands of the nations (Zephaniah 2:11 *RSVCE*)." This prophecy is fulfilled in New Testament, above all by the celebration of the Mass throughout the world where "No longer are people bidden to go up to Jerusalem, but each one shall remain in his own home and offer this worship."[85]

Section Questions

1. According to Zephaniah, to God "shall bow down, each in its place, all the lands of the nations (Zephaniah 2:11 *RSVCE*)." God also tells Zephaniah, "Yes, at that time I will change the speech of the peoples to a pure speech, that all of them may call on the name of the LORD and serve him with one accord (Zephaniah 3:9 *RSVCE*)." How did Fulgentius and Chrysostom interpret these prophecies in relationship to the Sacraments?

---

[84] Alberto Ferreiro, *Ancient Christian Commentary on Scripture, Old Testament XIV, The Twelve Prophets* (Downers Grove: InterVarsity Press, 2003), 355. Fulgentius of Ruspe's *To Monimus*, 2.5.1 is cited.

[85] Ferreiro, 355. John Chrysostom's *Demonstration Against the Pagans* 6.9 is cited.

10. Haggai

Haggai is the first of the three minor prophets who preached after the Judean people had returned to their homeland from living in exile in Babylon. The three prophets are traditionally ordered as the last of the twelve minor prophets. The three are Haggai, Zechariah, and Malachi. The book of Ezra names both Haggai and Zechariah as prophesying to the Jewish people who had returned to Judah. Heeding the prophecies, the Jerusalem Temple was restored under the supervision of the governor of Jerusalem, Zerubbabel (Ezra 5:1-2).

The Jewish people were released from Babylonian oppression when the Babylonians were defeated by the Persian Empire, led by King Cyrus the Great (c. 600-530 B.C.). According to the second book of Chronicles, "the LORD stirred up the spirit (2 Chronicles 36:22 *RSVCE*)" of King Cyrus to

---

[86] James Tissot (1836-1902), French painter / Public domain, "Haggai (watercolor circa 1896–1902 by James Tissot)," https://commons. wikimedia.org/wiki/File:Tissot_Haggai.jpg.

issue a proclamation that allowed the Jewish people to return to Judea and rebuild their holy Temple. King Cyrus's decree was honored by his successors, including, explain Bergsma and Pitre, by "his son Cambyses (530-522 B.C.) and Darius I (522-486 B.C., a Persian aristocrat who took the throne when Cambyses died childless."[87] The Temple was not completed and dedicated until King Artaxerxes's reign (possibly Artaxerxes I 465-424 B.C.).[88] Ezra records that that obedient to the "prophesying of Haggai ... and Zechariah" the Jewish people "finished their building by command of the God of Israel and by the decree of Cyrus and Darius and Artaxerxes King of Persia (Ezra 6:14 *RSVCE*)." Once the Temple was rebuilt and dedicated, the Jewish people restored the celebration of Passover (Ezra 6:19-22).

Haggai's name reflects the importance of celebrating the Passover and other Holy Days. In Hebrew his name is based on the word for a celebration, especially for a liturgical celebration *chag* (חג).[89] Haggai fulfilled the meaning of his name by calling his people to rebuild the Temple and there to restore liturgical worship. In his promotion of liturgical worship, Haggai does not denounce hypocritical worship, as other prophets did, such as Hosea with, "I desire mercy and not sacrifice, the knowledge of God, rather than burnt offerings (Hosea 6:6 *RSVCE*)." The difference between Haggai's and Hosea's prophecies does not mean that they cannot be reconciled with one another. Rather, their differences are complementary and are suited for different times, conformed to the different needs of the different times.

Hosea prophesied centuries before the Temple was destroyed in 586 B.C. At the time, what was needed to be prophesied against was hypocritical worship, in which those worshipping used worship to cloak and rationalize their abuse of the poor and other immoral behavior. Haggai prophesied after

---

[87] John Bergsma and Brant Pitre, *A Catholic Introduction to the Bible, Volume I* (San Francisco: Ignatius Press, 2018), 20308.

[88] Bergsma and Pitre, 455.

[89] "2282. chag," biblehub.com, https://biblehub.com/hebrew/2282.htm.

the Temple was destroyed and after the Jewish people were allowed to return to their homeland where they could rebuild their temple. During Haggai's time what was needed was a prophet who would encourage liturgical worship, with the implicit understanding, that for this worship to be pleasing to God the worshippers' life needed to also be a pleasing sacrifice to God. The sacrifice involved sacrificing excessive self-love and by demonstrating their love of God by justly loving their brothers and sisters, especially the poorest and marginalized.

The differences between Hosea and Haggai and between all the Twelve Minor Prophets are examples of what Pope Francis referred to as "a diversity 'reconciled' by the Holy Spirit" who "creates the diversity of charismata and then makes harmony of the charismata."[90] In explaining the reason for this "multiplicity and variety" Pope Francis cites Aquinas who teaches:

> that the distinction and multitude of things come from the intention of the first agent, who is God. For He brought things into being in order that His goodness might be communicated to creatures, and be represented by them; and because His goodness could not be adequately represented by one creature alone, He produced many and diverse creatures, that what was wanting to one in the representation of the divine goodness might be supplied by another. For goodness, which in God is simple and uniform, in creatures is manifold and divided and hence the whole universe together participates the divine goodness more perfectly, and represents it better than any single creature whatever.[91]

---

[90] Francis, "Reconciled Diversity," ewtn.com, https://www.ewtn.com/catholicism/library/reconciled-diversity-13103.

[91] Thomas Aquinas, "Summa Theologiae, First Part, Question 47, Article 1," newadvent.org, https://www.newadvent.org/summa/1047.htm.

When this teaching of Aquinas and Pope Francis are applied to prophetic literature, it may be asserted that the differences between various biblical prophets are intended by God to, borrowing words from Pope Francis, "complement one another in [their] ... partial reception of reality."[92]

Haggai's prophecy on rebuilding the Jerusalem Temple and restoring liturgical worship is in four oracles. In the first oracle (Haggai 1:1-15), God, through Haggai, commands the Jewish returnees to prioritize rebuilding the Jerusalem Temple over rebuilding and beautifying their personal homes. When the Jewish people returned to their homeland, they did not prioritize rebuilding the God's earthly home, the Jerusalem Temple, but rather focused on rebuilding their own homes. Challenging this disorder, God asks, "Is it time for you yourselves to dwell in your paneled houses?" God then points out that the Jerusalem Temple, God's house, "lies in ruin (Haggai 1:4 RSVCE)." Under the governorship of Zerubbabel, the people in Jerusalem "obey the voice of the LORD their God, and the words of Haggai (Haggai 1:12-15 RSVCE)."

In the second oracle (2:1-9), Haggai prophecies of an end of times where God will "shake the heavens and the earth (2:6 RSVCE)." This will be followed by the building of a future temple that "shall be greater than the former (Haggai 2:9 RSVCE)." Augustine interprets this prophecy as fulfilled in the Catholic Church which is made up of living stones as the First Letter of Peter describes, "you also, like living stones, are being built into a spiritual house to be a holy priesthood, offering spiritual sacrifices acceptable to God through Jesus Christ (1 Peter 2:5 RSVCE)."[93] The Letter to the Hebrews also interprets Haggai's prophecy as fulfilled in the Kingdom of God brought by

---

[92] Francis, "Apostolic Exhortation, *Evangelii Gaudium*, 24 November, 2013," vatican.va, http://www.vatican.va/content/francesco/en/apost_exhortations/documents/papa-francesco_esortazione-ap_20131124_evangelii-gaudium.html, Footnote 44.

[93] Ferreiro, 355. Augustine's *City of God* 18.48 is cited.

Jesus Christ (Hebrews 12:26). Jesus' death on the cross can be understood as fulfilling the shaking of the heavens and earth prophesied by Haggai for at Jesus' death "the earth shook and the rocks were split; the tombs also were opened, and many bodies of the saints who had fallen asleep were raised (Matthew 27:51-52 *RSVCE*)." After rising from the dead, and appearing to his disciples, Jesus sent the Holy Spirit down upon his disciples, and the Church was born. On that day of Pentecost, the Church was born and consists of "living stones" as a Temple of Jesus' presence.

The third oracle (Haggai 2:10-19) promises the Jewish people in Judah that their reprioritizing their life around worship of God, as represented by the building of the Temple, will be blessed by God. Haggai concludes with a brief fourth oracles (2:20-23) where God once again warns that the heavens and the earth will be shaken. "On that day" of judgment, prophecies Haggai, Zerubbabel will become God's chosen "signet ring (Haggai 2:23 *RSVCE*)." According to Ambrose, this prophecy is fulfilled by a soul who in repentance turn to Jesus and "receive Christ like a signet ring upon her, for she is the image of God."[94]

Section Questions

1. Name the three Minor Prophets who preached to the Judeans after they returned home from their exile in Babylon.
2. Who was King Cyrus and why were the Jewish people able to return to their homeland to rebuild their Temple during Cyrus's reign?
3. What is the Hebrew word that Haggai's name is based on, what does it mean, and how does this word directly relate to Hosea's prophecies?
4. With respect to Temple and liturgical worship how do Hosea and

---

[94] Ferreiro, 355. Ambrose's *Commentary on Tatian's Diatessaron* 3.10 is cited.

Haggai differ and complement one another?

5. In his second oracle, Haggai prophecies an end of times where God will "shake the heavens and the earth (Haggai 2:6 *RSVCE*)." Afterwards, a future temple will be built that "shall be greater than the former (Haggai 2:9 *RSVCE*)." How can these prophecies be understood as fulfilled after Jesus' death on the cross and at Pentecost?

11. Zechariah

Introduction

As presented in Ezra, Zechariah prophesied at the same time that Haggai prophesied (Ezra 5:1). The book of Zechariah provides specific dates for three oracles of Zechariah. These dates are given according to the year and month of the Persian King Darius I's reign (522-486 B.C.,). This manner of dating corresponds to the Christian Gregorian Calendar as follows, comment Bergsma and Pitre: "'Second year, eighth month of Darius' (Zech. 1:1-6) = 520 B.C. 2. 'Twenty fourth day of the eleventh month in the second year of Darius' (Zech. 1:7) = 519 B.C. 3. 'Fourth year of King Darius . . . fourth day of the ninth month.' (Zech. 7:1) = 518 B.C."[95]

If the Zechariah "son of Iddo (Zechariah 1:1 *RSVCE*)" is the same as the Zechariah "son of Iddo (Nehemiah 12:16 *RSVCE*)" then the prophet Zechariah was also a priest because the Zechariah referred to in Nehemiah is listed as a priest. In support of this, Jerome writes that the prophet Jeremiah "was from Anathoth, which is up to today a village three miles distant from

---

[95] John Bergsma and Brant Pitre, *A Catholic Introduction to the Bible, Volume I* (San Francisco: Ignatius Press, 2018), Kindle Location 20338.

Jerusalem, a priest from priests."[96]

Zechariah's role as a priest can help to explain why Zechariah and Haggai, whom Jerome also identified as a priest, focused their attention on restoring the Temple and Temple worship.[98] The importance of the Temple in Zechariah is evident in Zechariah's first vision and last chapter. In the first vision, God promises that "my house shall be built (Zechariah 1:16 *RSVCE*)" in Jerusalem. In the last chapter, Zechariah concludes by prophesying of a time when people from all nations will go up to Jerusalem "to keep the feast

---

[96] "Jerome, Prologue to Jeremiah (2006), translated by Keven P. Edgecomg" tertullian.org, http://www.tertullian.org/fathers/jerome_preface_jeremiah.htm.

[97] James Tissot / Public domain, "Zechariah as depicted by James Tissot," https://commons.wikimedia.org/wiki/File:Tissot_Zechariah.jpg.

[98] Bergsma and Pitre, Kindle Location 20279.

of booths (Zechariah 14:16 *RSVCE*)."

All the chapters may be divided into two parts, comment Bergsma and Pitre. The first part (Zechariah 1-8) are prophecies and visions on the present times in respect to the Temple and the Jewish people. The second part (Zechariah 9-14) are prophecies on the end times, the time of the Messiah and the Judgement of the LORD.[99]

Section Questions

1. According to Jerome was Zechariah a priest and if Jerome is correct why does this help to explain what Zechariah focuses on in his prophecies?

Prophecies on the Present Times Chapters 1-8

Chapters one through eight contain eight visions that are followed by a warning on fasting that is not accompanied by kindness and mercy especially for "the widow, the fatherless, the sojourner, or the poor (Zechariah 7:10 *RSVCE*)." In the last chapter of the section, God reassures that despite the sins of His people, "I will save my people…they shall be my people and I will be their God (Zechariah 8:7-8 *RSVCE*)." This time of salvation will coincide with joyful fasting, fasting that is joyful since it is no longer hypocritical, and therefore cold, but it is warm since it is formed by love, kindness and mercy with preferential care for those on the fringes on society, as commanded by God (Zechariah 8:18-19).

The eight visions that precede the joyful conclusion of the first section include the following: Four Horsemen (First Vision), Four Horns and Smiths (Second Vision), Measuring Line (Third Vision), Joshua Accused by Satan (Fourth Vision), Lampstand and Two Olive Trees (Fifth Vision), Flying

---

[99] Bergsma and Pitre, Kindle Location 20349.

Scroll (Sixth Vision), Woman Sitting in a Container (Seventh Vision), and Four Chariots (Eight Vision).

The first vision of four horsemen are also referred to in the last book of the bible, Revelation (6:1-2). The vision represents the trials and tribulations that human beings will experience in the end of times. Ezekiel calls these trials and tribulations "four sore acts of judgment, sword, famine, evil beasts, and pestilence (Ezekiel 14:21)" that are sent upon Jerusalem to purify the people of Jerusalem.

The second vision also contains four punishments but in the form of horns.

In the third vision, Zechariah sees a man measuring Jerusalem. He hears an angel say that Jerusalem will no longer have walls for in place of walls God will "be to her a wall of fire round about… and will be the glory within her (Zechariah 2:5 *RSVCE*)." This can be understood as fulfilled in the heavenly

---

[100] Viktor Mikhailovich Vasnetsov / Public domain, "*Four Horsemen of the Apocalypse*, an 1887 painting by Viktor Vasnetsov. From left to right are Death, Famine, War, and Conquest; the Lamb is at the top." https://commons.wikimedia.org/wiki/File:Apocalypse_vasnetsov.jpg.

Jerusalem prophesied in Revelation (21:9-27). Cyril of Jerusalem interprets the vision as fulfilled in Christ who was sent by the heavenly Father to dwell in our midst: "[F]or behold, I come and I will dwell in the midst of you, says the Lord (Zechariah 2:10 *RSVCE*)."[101]

In the fourth vision, Joshua is accused by Satan. Joshua is accused while he is wearing "filthy garments (Zechariah 3:4 *RSVCE*)." An angel orders Joshua's dirty clothes to be removed from him and be clothed in clean garments. Church Fathers interpreted Joshua and his dirty clothes in reference to Jesus. According to Jerome, the vision is fulfilled in Jesus whose dirty clothes were "our sins; he was wrapped up in the folds of our vices."[102] Our sins, our "dirty clothes" are removed, comments Gregory of Nyssa, by Baptism. Baptism allows us to participate in Christ's sacrificial, cleansing love.[103]

The fifth vision is of a golden lampstand flanked by two olive trees. Revelation contains a similar vision of "two olive trees and two lampstands which stand before the Lord of the earth (11:4 *RSVCE*)."

The flying scroll of the sixth vision bears on it warning of punishment of those who persist in sin.

The seventh vision then depicts sin in the form of a woman sitting in a container that has a heavy leaden cover over it. In commenting on the heavy leaden cover trapping the woman, Gregory of Nyssa writes, "For virtue is something light and exhilarating. All who live according to it 'fly along the clouds,' ... but sin is heavy [like] ... a 'talent of lead.'"[104]

The visions conclude with an eighth vision similar to the first one of four

---

[101] Alberto Ferreiro, *Ancient Christian Commentary on Scripture, Old Testament XIV, The Twelve Prophets* (Downers Grove: InterVarsity Press, 2003), 359. Cyril of Jerusalem's *Dialogue with Trypho*137.

[102] Ferreiro, 359. Gregory of Nyssa's *On the Baptism of Christ* is cited.

[103] Ferreiro, 359. Jerome's *Homilies on the Psalms* 36 is cited.

[104] Ferreiro, 365. Gregory of Nyssa *On Virginity* 18.

horsemen, but this time Zechariah sees four chariots.

Section Questions

1. Choose one of the following visions and explain how they may be interpreted as fulfilled in the New Testament. 1st - 4 Horsemen, 2nd 4 Horns and Smiths, 3rd Measuring Line, 4th Joshua Accused by Satan, 5th Lampstand and Two Olive Trees, 6th Flying Scroll, 7th Woman Sitting in a Container, 8th 4 Chariots

---

Prophecies on the End Times Chapters 9-14

Chapter nine contains a prophecy of restored Jerusalem. According to the prophecy, a king of Jerusalem will ride into the city "triumphant and victorious…humble and riding on a donkey, on a colt the foal of a donkey … and he shall command peace to the nations (Zechariah 9:9-10 *RSVCE*)." The Gospel of Matthew quotes and interprets this prophecy along with a similar prophecy in Isaiah (62:11). In Matthew, the prophecy is fulfilled by Jesus when Jesus rode into Jerusalem on a donkey and on a colt (Matthew 21:1-7). Church Fathers interpreted the colt and donkey as representing Gentiles and Jewish believers who will carry the Good News of Jesus to the world.[106]

Chapter ten continues the theme of the restoration, by prophesying the restoration of both kingdoms: Southern Kingdom of Judah and Northern Kingdom of Israel. Before promising the restoration, God says that his "anger is hot against the shepherds, and I will punish the leaders (Zechariah 10:3 *RSVCE*)." This is followed by a prophecy of a holy leader who will become "the cornerstone (Zechariah 10:4 *RSVCE*)." Isaiah also contains a similar prophecy of a cornerstone (Isaiah 28:16) as does Psalm 118. Quoting verse twenty-two of Psalm 118, the First Letter of Peter identifies Jesus with the cornerstone that the "the builders rejected (1 Peter 2:7 *RSVCE*)." Jesus is the cornerstone who was rejected and yet at the same time is the chosen one of God to bring salvation to Israel, and, through Israel, to the whole world.

Chapter ten's prophecy of Israel's restoration is followed by chapter eleven which warns of a "worthless shepherd, who deserts the flock (Zechariah 11:17 *RSVCE*)."

Chapter twelve then describes a victorious but repentant Jerusalem

---

[106] Alberto Ferreiro, *Ancient Christian Commentary on Scripture, Old Testament XIV, The Twelve Prophets* (Downers Grove: InterVarsity Press, 2003), Kindle Location 8356-8422.

whose inhabitants "look on him whom they have pierced" and "mourn for him (Zechariah 12:10 *RSVCE*)." Church Fathers understood this verse as referring to Jesus' death on the cross.[107]

In a similar vein of thought, chapter thirteen describes a shepherd who is struck. Leaderless, the sheep are scattered (Zechariah 13:7). Matthew records Jesus quoting these words of Zechariah as Jesus walked with his Apostles to pray in the Garden of Gethsemane shortly before being betrayed by Judas (Matthew 26:31).

Zechariah concludes by describing the "day of the Lord (Zechariah 14:1 *RSVCE*)" when the Lord will become king over all the earth (Zechariah 14:9 *RSVCE*)." People from all nations will come to Jerusalem "to worship the King, the LORD of hosts, and to keep the feasts of booths (Zechariah 14:16 *RSVCE*)." This feast is also at times translated the feast of tabernacles and refers to the Jewish feast of Sukkot (סֻכּוֹת). As stipulated in Leviticus, this feast lasts for seven days during which the Jewish people are to live in tents, which commemorate the time their ancestors fled Egypt and lived in tents (Leviticus 23:42-43). According to Bergsma and Pitre, Jesus, "became flesh and dwelt among us (John 1:14 *RSVCE*)" is the ultimate fulfillment of this prophecy. This is particularly evident when the original Greek of the New Testament is looked at. The Greek word for "dwelt" is *eskenosen* (ἐσκήνωσεν), from the verb *skénoó* (σκηνόω), which literally means "to pitch or live in a tent".[108] A most fitting title for Jesus, therefore, is "Emmanuel" for in Hebrew the name Emmanuel (Isaiah 7:14) means God is with us. Jesus is with us since as God He has pitched His tent in human flesh.

---

[107] Alberto Ferreiro, *Ancient Christian Commentary on Scripture, Old Testament XIV, The Twelve Prophets* (Downers Grove: InterVarsity Press, 2003), Kindle Location 8735-8792.

[108] "4637. skénoó," bible.hub.com, https://biblehub.com/greek/4637.htm.

Section Questions

1. According to Matthew's Gospel, how does Jesus fulfill Zechariah's chapter nine prophecy of a future king riding on colt and donkey and what, according to Church Fathers, do the colt and donkey spiritually represent?

2. Zechariah's last chapter prophecies a time when people from all nations will journey to Jerusalem "to worship the King, the LORD of hosts, and to keep the feasts of booths (Zechariah 14:16 *RSVCE*)." How is this fulfilled by the Incarnation? Include in your response the following: Feast of Booths, Tents, "And the Word became flesh and dwelt among us (John 1:14)."

12. Malachi

The book of Malachi contains the prophecies of the third minor prophet who preached after the Judean people had been freed by the Persians to return home. Traditionally, it is considered to be the last of the prophetic books, and, as a result, serves as a bridge between the Old Testament and New Testament.[109] It was likely composed sometime between 500 B.C. – 450 B.C.[110] It is not clear who the prophet of writing is since the Hebrew word Malachi (מַלְאָכִי), means "my messenger," and, according to McConville, is not used in the Old Testament as a name for anyone.[111] McConville also points out that in chapter three the word *malaki* "appears in 3:1, where it is

---

[109] John Bergsma and Brant Pitre, *A Catholic Introduction to the Bible, Volume I* (San Francisco: Ignatius Press, 2018), Kindle Location 20465.

[110] Bergsma and Pitre, Kindle Location 20465.

[111] Gordon J. McConville, *Exploring the Old Testament: A Guide to the Prophets: 4 Exploring the Bible Series* (Downers Grove: InterVarsity Press, 2002), 259.

always translated 'my messenger,'" indicating that this word is very likely not intended to be a name for a specific prophet.[112]

[113]

The messenger in the book acts on God's behalf to purify the people "till they present right offerings to the Lord (Malachi 3:3 *RSVCE*)." Throughout the body of the book, Malachi (my messenger) presents the arguments of the people against God's ways and then defends God's manner of relating to the people of Judah. In chapter one, Malachi presents the people's defense "You say, 'How have we despised your [God's] name?" Malachi then counters this defensive question with a response that is intended to elicit self-accusation, repentance and a turning back to God by joining right action with right

---

[112] McConville, 259.

[113] James Tissot (1836-1902), French painter / Public domain, "Malachi (watercolor circa 1896–1902 by James Tissot)," https://commons. wikimedia.org/wiki/File:Tissot_Malachi.jpg.

worship. Malachi's counter is, "By offering polluted food upon my altar (Malachi 1:7 *RSVCE*)." He then proceeds to bring up other similar claims and counters each one in defense of God's ways and judgments. This pattern of claim and counter can be broken into six distinct arguments (Malachi 1:2-3:15), note Bergsma and Pitre, that are followed by a verse on repentance (Malachi 3:16) and a conclusion where God comforts and teaches the remaining people of Judah (Malachi 3:17-4:6).[114]

In the conclusion, Malachi commands his people, to "Remember the law of my servant Moses, the statutes and ordinances that I commanded him at Horeb for all Israel (Malachi 4:1)." The book then closes with God's promise to send "Elijah the prophet before the great and awesome day of the LORD (Malachi 4:5 *RSVCE*)." With these verses, Malachi affirms the mutually supportive relationship between the law, represented by Moses, and prophetic literature, represented by Elijah. In Jesus, the law and the prophets perfectly come together. In union with the prophets, Jesus called an end to hypocritical worship, for example, when Jesus quoted Hosea to the Pharisees, "I desire mercy, and not sacrifice (Matthew 9:13 *RSVCE*)."

When this verse is interpreted in its Scriptural context it becomes evident that Jesus is not emphasizing mercy as a replacement for law and sacrifice, for Jesus teaches, "I say to you, till heaven and earth pass away, not an iota, not a dot, will pass from the law until all is accomplished (Matthew 5:18 *RSVCE*)." Similar to Malachi, who affirms both the law and the prophets Jesus also instructs, "Do not think that I have come to abolish the law and the prophets; I have come not to abolish them but to fulfil them (Matthew 5:17 *RSVCE*)."

The fulfillment of the priestly laws, especially those concerning sacrifice, is encountered in Jesus Christ the one true high priest. As Benedict XVI explains, "Christ, who makes an offering of himself on the Cross, is the true high priest, anticipated symbolically by the Aaronic priesthood. Hence his

---

[114] Bergsma and Pitre, Kindle Location 20517.

self-giving – his obedience, which takes us all up and brings us back to God – is the true worship, the true sacrifice."[115] Because of Christ's perfect sacrifice as both the unblemished victim and the sinless priest, "the whole world" is, explains Benedict XVI, drawn by God into Christ's perfect sacrificial, priestly love "in such a way that everyone together with him becomes an offering that is 'acceptable, sanctified by the Holy Spirit (Rom 15:16.'"[116]

Malachi's prophecy of a "pure offering (Malachi 1:11 *RSVCE*)" that will be offered in every place is fulfilled in the offering of the Holy Mass, the Eucharist, in which under the appearance of bread and wine the one priest, Jesus Christ is offered to his Heavenly Father in the love of the Holy Spirit. This fulfillment in Christ becomes clearer when the Hebrew word for offering is examined. The Hebrew word for "offering" is *minhah* (מִנְחָה) which is usually used in the Bible in reference to bread/grain offerings. In the context of this passage, comment Bergsma and Pitre, the *minhah* is a bread offering that along with all other sacrifices are to be offered only in the one place designated by God for sacrificial offerings, which became the Jerusalem Temple (Deuteronomy 12:2-7). In this chapter of Deuteronomy, multiple places of worship are identified with pagan worship and, hence, are commanded to be destroyed.

In contrast with Deuteronomy's restriction to one place of worship, Malachi prophecies of a time where a "pure" and therefore acceptable sacrifice to God will be offered in every place, which implies that even in Gentle lands a pure, bread offering will be offered. In equating this perfect bread offering with the Eucharist, Augustine teaches, "Now if we see that everywhere in our time, 'from the rising of the sun to the going down thereof

---

[115] Joseph Ratzinger, *Jesus of Nazareth Part Two, Holy Week: From the Entrance into Jerusalem to the Resurrection,* trans. Vatican Secretariat of State (San Francisco: Ignatius Press, 2011), 237.

[116] Ratzinger, 238.

[Malachi 1:11],' this sacrifice is being offered by Christ's priests according to the order of Melchizedek."[117]

"Christ's priests" is a reference to the participation of Christians in the one priesthood of Jesus Christ in a hierarchical manner, one which is similar but also essentially different from the Levitical priesthood of the Old Testament. It is similar in that there is a threefold ministry of bishops, priests and deacons that is patterned upon the threefold ministry of the high priest, the priests (the Kohanim related to Aaron the first high priest), and the Levites (who were not related to Aaron). It is different in that the New Testament almost exclusively uses the Greek term for priest (*hiereus*, ἱερεύς, ἕως, ὁ) for the Jewish priests and for Jesus as the priest, especially as the "high priest forever according to the order of Melchizedek (Hebrews 6:20 *RSVCE*)." As Benedict XVI clearly affirms, quoting Schelkle, the New Testament:

> never calls the officials "priests", or the office "office". The Greek words for office (*arkhe, exousia, time, telos*) are not, for the New Testament, appropriate descriptions for the offices of the Church.
>
> ... One can in no way identify the New Testament office, which is in fact New Testament service, with the phenomenon of priesthood in other religions. It is by nature something totally different. That it resembles priesthood factually, purely as a phenomenon, does not derive from its nature, but from the fact that a perfect fulfillment of being in the world of concrete appearances always remains impossible. It comes from a breaking in of the individual element which is not of Christ. So it is that, to this day, the sixth sacrament is called, in the language of the Church, not

---

[117] Alberto Ferreiro, *Ancient Christian Commentary on Scripture, Old Testament XIV, The Twelve Prophets* (Downers Grove: InterVarsity Press, 2003), Kindle Location 9273. Augustine's *City of God* 18.35 is cited.

sacerdotium, but *ordo*.

There is a further historical point to be made. The special character of the Christian office emerges with particular clarity when we compare the Christian apostle with his direct parallels in the history of religion, the rabbi and the *theios anthropos* ("man of God") of the Greeks. Both the latter have their own authority, whereas the essential thing for an apostle is to be a servant of Christ and, like Christ, to live by the motto, "My teaching is not mine, but his who sent me" (Jn 7:16). Thus, the sense of mission for the rabbi and the "man of God" is an awareness of self; for the apostle it is an awareness of service. [Quoting Schelkle] "The rabbi's pupil has the goal of becoming a master himself. But for Jesus' disciple, discipleship is not a beginning; it is the fulfillment and destination of his life. He always remains a disciple."

We might add that, as a "father", he still remains a "brother"; his fatherly office is a form of brotherly service, and nothing else.[118]

With that stated, it is important to note along with Albert Vanhoye and Jean Galot that although St. Paul does not call himself a priest he does

---

[118] Joseph Ratzinger, *The Meaning of Christian Brotherhood* (San Francisco: Ignatius Press, 1993), 61-62. Ratzinger quotes Schelkle "The New Testament knows these words but does not employ them in the realm of the Church; rather it draws on the word *diakonia. Arkhe* is restricted in New Testament usage to the authority of synagogue and state or to the angelic powers, *time* to the dignity of office of the Old Testament high priest. The result of such lexicographical investigation is impressive enough evidence that office in the Church is an institution essentially ordered to service. The result also makes manifest the self-understanding of the New Testament that order and law mean essentially different things in the Church and in the world. Therefore, they cannot be named with the same words."

describe himself as "a minister of Christ Jesus to the Gentiles in the priestly service of the gospel of God (Romans 15:16 *RSVCE*)."[119] With these words, comments T.J. Lane, "Paul does not merely compare himself with a Jewish priest; he realizes that he is a *leitourgos* and exercising priesthood coming from Christ."[120] In a similar vein of though, Benedict XVI clearly states:

> Through the sacramental ordination conferred by the imposition of hands and the consecratory prayers of the Bishop, "a specific ontological bond which unites the priest to Christ, High Priest and Good Shepherd" is established. Thus, the identity of the priest comes from the specific participation in the Priesthood of Christ, in which the one ordained becomes, in the Church and for the Church, a real, living and faithful image of Christ the Priest, "a sacramental representation of Christ, Head and Shepherd". Through consecration, the priest "receives a spiritual 'power' as a gift which is a participation in the authority with which Jesus Christ, through his Spirit, guides the Church".[121]

More simply put by Fr. Ronald D. Witherup, S.S., "Jesus is the perfect priest and victim. He replaces the Old Testament priesthood. There are no longer priests only one priest who is Jesus. We are presbyters Jesus is the only

---

[119] The Greek word for priestly service is *hierourgounta* (ἱερουργοῦντα).

[120] T.J. Lane, *The Catholic Priesthood: Biblical Foundations* (Steubenville, Emmaus Road Publishing, 2016), 154.

[121] Congregation for the Clergy, "Directory on the Ministry and Life of Priests, January 31, 1994," no. 2, vatican.va, http://www.vatican.va/roman_curia/congregations/cclergy/documents/rc_con_cclergy_doc_31011994_directory_en.html, (accessed December 17, 2016).

New Testament priest."[122] Deacons (servants), *presbyteroi*/priests (elders), and *episkipoi*/bishops (overseers) all participate in the one ministerial priesthood of Jesus Christ. This ministerial priesthood is complemented and joined by the "royal" or "common priesthood" of all the baptized as the *Catechism of the Catholic Church* instructs:

> The whole Church is a priestly people. Through Baptism all the faithful share in the priesthood of Christ. This participation is called the "common priesthood of the faithful." Based on this common priesthood and ordered to its service, there exists another participation in the mission of Christ: the ministry conferred by the sacrament of Holy Orders, where the task is to serve in the name and in the person of Christ the Head in the midst of the community (*CCC* 1591).[123]

All who participate in the one priesthood of Jesus Christ are to do so by emphasizing service to Jesus Christ and mutual service to one another in which ruling is of less importance than service, for as Benedict XVI writes, "the category that corresponds to the [New Testament] priesthood is not that of rule."[124] Rather the category that corresponds to the New Testament is service to the "sacred origin" who is Jesus Christ, who is the one priest.[125] Benedict XVI clarifies this with, "the priesthood has to be a conduit and a

---

[122] Ronald D. Witherup, "The Theology of Priesthood and Implications for Seminary Ministry," 13th Institute for Formators, Theological College, Washington, D.C. June 8th, Lecture Notes.

[123] "Catechism of the Catholic Church," vatican.va, http://www.vatican.va/archive/ccc_css/archive/catechism/p2s2c3a6.htm, no. 1591.

[124] Ratzinger, *Salt of the Earth*, trans. Adrian Walker (San Francisco: Ignatius Press, 1997), 190-191.

[125] Ratzinger, *Salt of the Earth*, 190-191.

making present of a beginning and has to make itself available for this task. When priesthood, episcopacy, and papacy are understood essentially in terms of rule, then things are truly wrong and distorted."[126]

An essential way where the one priesthood of Jesus Christ is made evident in the world is the participation of the baptized in Jesus' one priesthood during the celebration of the Eucharist, the fulfillment of the prophecy of Malachi that "from the rising of the sun to its setting" a "pure" bread offering will be offered (Malachi 1:11 *RSVCE*).

Another important way Malachi points to Jesus is his forceful prophecy on divorce. Divorce contradicts the absolutely faithful love of God to his people as sacramentally represented by Jesus offering himself to all in the Eucharist. Speaking on behalf of God, Malachi states, "For I hate divorce, says the LORD the God of Israel.... So take heed to yourselves and do not be faithless (Malachi 2:16 *RSVCE*)."

Jesus affirms Malachi's teaching by intensifying the demands of the Mosaic law with, "For your hardness of heart Moses allowed you to divorce your wives, but from the beginning it was not so. And I say to you: whoever divorces his wife, except for unchastity, and marries another, commits adultery (Matthew 19:8-9 *RSVCE*)." Focusing his attention on this hardness of heart, Malachi condemns Judean men who leave their wives to join themselves sinfully to younger, more physically attractive woman. After condemning this cold-hearted practices and disordered love, Malachi asserts, "let none be faithless to the wife of his youth (Malachi 2:15 *RSVCE*)." The ultimate reason against divorce is God's eternally faithful love to his people that marriages are to represent, and which are created ways by which people demonstrate their grateful love back to God by faithful love to those they are in a covenantal relationship with in their participation in the one priesthood of Jesus Christ.

---

[126] Ratzinger, *Salt of the Earth*, 190-191.

Section Questions

1. What does Malachi's name mean in Hebrew?
2. God tells Malachi, "from the rising of the sun to its setting my name is great among the nations, and in every place incense is offered to my name, and a pure offering (Malachi 1:11 *RSVCE*)." How may this prophecy be believed to be fulfilled in the Eucharist? Include in your response the following: *Minhah* offering, multiple places, single place of tent and Temple, Acceptable "pure offering".
3. Compare the Old Testament Priesthood with the New Testament Priesthood. Include the following in your response: High Priest, Kohanim, Levites, Use of Greek Term Priest in New Testament, Sacred Rule and Sacred Origin, "Pure Offering (Malachi 1:11)."

---

[127] Franciszek Żmurko / Public domain, "Illustration of the coming of God's Messenger in 3:1, by Franciszek Żmurko." https://commons. wikimedia.org/wiki/File:Gustave_Dor%C3%A9_Malachi%C3%A1%C5%A 1_3.1.jpg.